Inverted

TOM ELLSWORTH

inVerted

LIVING OUT THE PERSPECTIVE-CHANGING
PARABLES JESUS TOLD

Standard®
PUBLISHING

Cincinnati, Ohio

Published by Standard Publishing, Cincinnati, Ohio
www.standardpub.com

Also available: *Inverted Group Member Discussion Guide*, ISBN 978-0-7847-2926-7, copyright © 2011 by Standard Publishing

Printed in: United States of America
Acquisitions editor: Dale Reeves
Project editor: Laura Derico
Cover design: Thinkpen Design Inc., www.thinkpendesign.com
Interior design: Dina Sorn at Ahaa! Design

ISBN 978-0-7847-2925-0

Library of Congress Cataloging-in-Publication Data

Ellsworth, Tom, 1955-
  Inverted : living out the perspective-changing parables Jesus told / Tom Ellsworth.
    p. cm.
  Includes bibliographical references (p.   ).
  ISBN 978-0-7847-2925-0
  1. Jesus Christ--Parables. 2. Christian life. I. Title.
  BT375.3.E54 2011
  248.4--dc22
                              2010043732

16 15 14 13 12 11   1 2 3 4 5 6 7 8 9

For our granddaughter,
Addyson Jennifer Suhr.
Welcome to this world, precious one. I have so many stories to tell you.
Most of all, I can't wait to introduce you to the greatest Storyteller of all—
Jesus!

I never dreamed my story would be filled with so many wonderful people—I am rich indeed! Should I live to be a hundred, I will never be able to adequately express my thanks to all. Here are a few who have written the best parts of my story.

My wife, Elsie. After more than thirty-three years of marriage, I still marvel that she said yes. That she chose to share her life's story with me keeps me looking forward to each new chapter of our lives together. I am deeply grateful for her encouragement, wisdom, and inspiration. Without her love and patience I could never have completed this project.

My kids: Emily and Matt Crum and Rebekah and Errek Suhr. The most incredible chapter of my story has been the one entitled Dad. I can't imagine life without our daughters. And now they have added to my joy by bringing two great sons-in-law into our family.

My parents, Tom and Midge Ellsworth. I have wonderful parents who from the very beginning of my story have guided me with their faith, modeled a Christian home through their marriage, and challenged me to serve God. Their love is a gift.

My spiritual family at Sherwood Oaks Christian Church. For the last thirty years, I have been privileged to serve and worship with this great church. I am indebted to the leadership, staff, and congregation for their encouraging support. Even after three decades, they are still gracious listeners!

My editors, Dale Reeves and Laura Derico. Their kind words have kept me going, their editorial skills have strengthened my writing, and their insight has kept me focused. Thanks!

And you! Thank you for taking time to read this book. I hope the following pages will refresh your memory regarding the best stories ever told and will rekindle your passion to help turn an inverted world right side up with the gospel of Jesus Christ.

Acknowledgments

Contents

The photographer drove down the dusty road, scouring the country-side for a quaint old barn for the magazine's front cover. He spotted a barn that had played the role of a billboard in years past. The paint was badly faded but still legible. On the east side it read, "Chew Mail Pouch Tobacco" and on the opposite, "See Rock City." Unique, but not quite what he had in mind. He turned down a well-worn gravel lane and drove for miles. Just when he thought success had eluded him, he topped a rise in the road and there it was—the most picturesque barn he'd ever laid eyes on. He slowed to a stop, grabbed his camera, and began taking pictures as he walked. The barn was round, resting on a slight rise in the barn lot. Though older than the See Rock City barn, this one had been well maintained through the years. On the peak of the barn's roof rested a quaint cupola, with a weather vane that squawked on its rusty post as it twisted in the breeze. He zoomed in on the weather vane, and that's when he spotted the faint outline of words.

About that time the farmer ambled out through the barn door. The photographer excitedly explained his assignment and asked a few ques-tions about the barn's history. Then, pointing at the cupola he inquired, "I couldn't help but notice the words on the weather vane—*God is Faithful.* I'm not sure I understand. Are you saying that God's faithfulness is as fickle as the wind that blows?"

The old farmer leaned against the door, spit, and then responded, "Mis-ter, me and that barn have been here for a long time. I painted those words on the weather vane when I was fourteen years old. I'm now eighty-six and I can tell you that in the seventy-two years since, I have never found God to be fickle. That weather vane means that no matter what direction the wind blows in life, God is faithful."

I can shut my eyes and see that winding gravel road, the round barn, and the farmer who'd spent his entire life on that plot of ground. I love

Introduction

stories. Words create images that transform our minds into better theaters than Hollywood's silver screen. Stories are adventures that take us to places where we have never set foot. As a boy I traveled down the river on a flatboat with Huck Finn, searched for riches with Long John Silver on Treasure Island, and helped Sherlock Holmes solve baffling mysteries.

Stories are easy to remember and, consequently, so are the lessons or values they teach. You may not be good with quotes, equations, or theorems, but you can retell a story. From the beginning, God wired us to love stories. Long before papyrus, parchment, pens, and printing presses, history was passed along from generation to generation by storytelling. It's still one of the most powerful means of communication. Some of my fondest memories are of sitting with my grandparents and listening to the stories of a time period I could visit only in their memories. I will retell their stories to my grandchildren, who will in turn tell them again to future generations. In this day of information overload, some may conclude that storytelling is a thing of the past. I don't agree. A well-told story touches us in a personal way that no electronic means ever could. Storytelling has a lasting impact too. Try this experiment. Look at the following list of names:

- George Clinton
- Daniel Tompkins
- William King
- Thomas Hendricks
- James Sherman

Do you know what these men had in common? They all served as vice president of the United States. They were elected to the second highest office of the land and were only one breath away from the presidency, but most Americans are clueless about them or their contributions to advance our nation. Not much of a lasting impact, huh?

Let's try again. Can you identify what the following people share in common?

- Hans Christian Andersen
- Lewis Carroll

- Jacob and Wilhelm Grimm
- Laura Ingalls Wilder
- Charles Perrault

Storytellers! They told and/or wrote some of the most endearing tales we read as children. Their works will continue to thrill children of all ages for generations to come.

But there is one storyteller who simply has no peers—Jesus. If I could travel back in time, I would return to a day in the life of Christ to hear him teach about the kingdom of Heaven through the most incredible stories of all time. Others before and since have used stories in their teaching, but none compare to those told by Jesus. Even nonbelievers refer to humanitarians as Good Samaritans or speak of wayward friends as "returning prodigals." If only they knew the author of those incredible word pictures.

> Stories are adventures that take us to places where we have never set foot.

Jesus used simple and recognizable settings and commonplace things to teach profound, life-changing truths. His ordinary stories—his parables—impacted people in some extraordinary ways:

- Exposed their hypocrisy
- Challenged their spiritual thinking
- Incited their anger
- Touched their emotions
- Stirred their passions
- Motivated them to serve others
- Convicted them of their sin

Surely no one ever dozed off while Jesus taught!

Our English word *parable* has its etymological roots in the ancient Greek word *paraballo*, which means "to throw alongside."[1] Jesus threw these stories alongside the truth he sought to teach and they became the verbal vehicle to convey his message. Some consider a parable as merely a sermon illustration—but it is much more. Not all Jesus' parables fit neatly under a single definition. From narratives to metaphors and similes, his parables cover a wide spectrum of linguistic tools.

> Others before and since have used stories in their teaching, but none compare to those told by Jesus.

Categorizing Jesus' parables is not an easy task, especially since some may fit into more than one category. Here is a simple listing that will apply to most of his parables:

1. *True-to-life parables:* These stories came from everyday life and were easily identified by all who heard. Jesus' listeners had seen seed growing in a farmer's field, yeast at work in a batch of dough, or a sheep wandering off from the shepherd's flock. Jesus used self-evident truths to explore the challenges of human nature and daily living.

2. *Event-based parables:* These stories used a specific past event to teach a present truth. Consider the parables of the woman whose persistent pleas before the judge finally convinced him to administer justice (Luke 18:1-8), or the farmer who (after his crop began to grow) discovered that an enemy had sown weeds in his field (Matthew 13:24-30).

3. *Model parables:* These stories challenged the listener's behavior with the example of another's. The Good Samaritan and the Pharisee and the Tax Collector are model parables that focus directly on the character of an individual with examples to be either imitated or avoided.

4. *"How much more" parables:* These stories contrast the character of imperfect humans with a perfect God. "How much more" parables demonstrate that God's actions far exceed our human attempts. Jesus set the stage for such a contrast by affirming that no caring father would give his child a snake if the child asked for a fish. Then he added, "If

you then, though you are evil, know how to give good gifts to your children, how much more will your Father in heaven give the Holy Spirit to those who ask him" (Luke 11:13).

5. *Parabolic sayings:* These are often simple, one-statement truths that the Gospel writers identified as a parable. For instance, "He also told them this parable: 'Can a blind man lead a blind man? Will they not both fall into a pit?'" (Luke 6:39). Proverbial in nature, these simple statements convey profound truths.[2]

Christ's parables have also been classified according to moral lessons and truths they communicate:

- *Nine* advance the responsibility of stewardship or good management.
- *Nine* show the importance of obedience as a habit of a devoted heart.
- *Eight* examine the history of the kingdom in this present age.
- *Six* highlight the beauty of forgiveness and selfless love.
- *Five* specifically set forth God's divine character and attributes.
- *Four* challenge the disciple to be perpetually watchful.
- *Three* confront the need for consistency in teaching and behavior.
- *Three* advance humbleness and genuineness in prayer.
- *One* focuses on the necessity of humility in our relationship with God.[3]

Regardless of how they are categorized, all parables share this in common—they each teach one specific truth. Interpret each parable in light of its context: linguistic, historical, social, and spiritual. When studying the parables, avoid seeing them as allegories where every descriptive phrase holds some symbolic implication. John Bunyan's classic work, *Pilgrim's Progress*, is exactly that—an allegory. Every twist of the road or every character that Christian encounters along the way is an allegorical lesson.

The barn story at the beginning of this introduction is like a parable in that it teaches one main point—God is faithful. If, when you read the story, you thought that there was hidden meaning in the fact that the barn was round or that the number seventy-two seemed biblically symbolic or that I was endorsing a visit to Rock City, then you made the story far more complicated than I intended. I just want you to know that you can count on the Lord no matter what! Be careful not to make a similar mistake with Jesus' parables. I like how Lloyd John Ogilvie put it: "The parables are like a ball of yarn with one single strand protruding. Get hold of that, and you can unravel the whole ball."[4]

As you make your way through this book, watch for that single strand of truth. These stories of Jesus are truly life-changing; when taken to heart they will help you become grateful, compassionate, forgiving, gracious, faithful, authentic, perceptive, and vigilant. Here's something else these parables of Jesus all have in common—*inverted* conclusions. Filled with twists and surprises, not one of them ended as the crowd expected. I suspect several of Jesus' listeners walked away muttering, "Didn't see *that* coming." That's not to suggest that Jesus' followers were dull—to the contrary, we simply have the advantage of 2,000 years of interpretation. Armed with our assumptions, opinions, and predisposed ideas, we are just as easily caught off guard. Consider the following: Once upon a time, a man left home to go jogging. He jogged for a while and then made a left turn. Picking up his pace, he jogged on before turning left again. Eventually, after he jogged a while longer, he turned left one more time. Home was in sight as he jogged on, but when he arrived back at home, he was met by two masked men.

Based on the information above, answer these questions:

1. Why did the man leave home to go jogging?
2. Who were the masked men?

Give up? Check out the answer below.*

Surprise! Didn't see *that* coming, did you? Some of us have become so familiar with the parables of Jesus that we hardly pause to consider how un-expected and powerful they were when first heard. They turned the world of the first century upside down; or perhaps I should say, in an inverted world culture these truths of God turned it right side up. So set aside what you think you know of his stories and rediscover these fabulous parables from the greatest storyteller of all time.

---

* The man jogged from home because he had just hit a home run in a baseball game. The masked men were the catcher and the umpire.

Gratitude is a sometime thing in this world. Just because you've been feeding them all winter, don't expect the birds to take it easy on your grass seed.
—Bill Vaughan, in the *Kansas City Star*

My grandparents lived on a forty-acre farm in the rolling hills of southern Indiana. The old barn sagged and the rusty tin roof leaked in spots, but walking through the door was like entering a different world. New adventures beckoned from the hayloft and corncrib. The barn's weathered oak siding had wrinkled and narrowed with the passing of time, allowing ribbons of sunlight to filter through. If you looked closely you could see the dust dancing.

The garden-fresh food had a taste all its own; nothing fancy but always scrumptious. Grandma cooked on a cast-iron, wood-burning stove, and the aroma of her fresh-baked bread filled the kitchen with an invitation "to come and sit for a spell." I loved the farm; I found myself drawn to its quiet simplicity and ageless beauty. Maybe that's why I worked part-time in high school for a local farmer. Perhaps that's why I raised three acres of soybeans one summer to help buy an engagement ring. Maybe that's why I

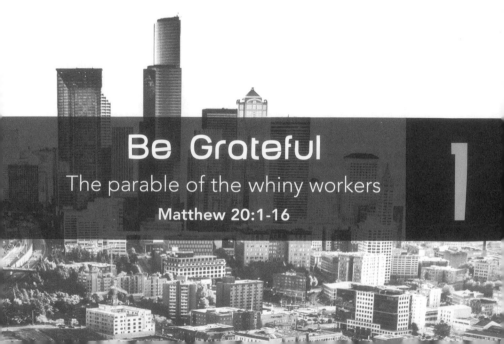

Be Grateful
The parable of the whiny workers
Matthew 20:1-16

1

have always enjoyed visiting my in-laws in Illinois—they too are farmers.

I believe the Judean farmers of the first century were near to the heart of Jesus. After all, they worked the land that *he* had created. They tilled the soil, planted the seed, picked the fruit, and celebrated the harvest just like Adam had done at the very beginning of time. Could that be why Jesus used a farm as the setting for many of his parables?

Life on the Farm

In one of his stories, Jesus spoke of a farmer who sowed seed (Matthew 13:1-23). I have it pictured this way: With the opening words of the parable, Jesus pointed to a farmer actually planting his field within sight of the audience. He sowed truths in the hearts of his listeners as the sweat-soaked farmer moved up and down the rows, scattering handfuls of seed.

The soils represented the hearts of people; the seed represented God's Word. Some seed fell along the hardened footpath where hungry birds quickly gobbled it up. At times the Word falls on hard hearts and deaf ears—before it can begin its penetrating work, the evil one swoops in and devours it. Other seed found a home in the rocky ground. The seed germinated in the thin top layer of soil, but could not be sustained with such shallow roots. Some people receive the Word eagerly, but it never really takes root in their hearts. And again, some of the seed dropped into ground shared with weeds. As the good seed gained a roothold, the nasty weeds also sprang up and hogged the sunlight, soaking up any moisture and leaving no room for the good plants to grow. There are those who desperately need the Word, but the problems of life—like worthless weeds—crowd out any harvest of hope. God's Word never has a chance in their hearts. Some other seed, however, found its way into the properly prepared earth and returned a wonderful harvest in the months to come. And so it is with God's Word: when planted in the right heart, the eternal harvest is great.

In another story Jesus introduced a well-to-do farmer whose harvest was so plentiful, he concluded his only option was to tear down his barns and build bigger ones (Luke 12:13-21). Talk about extreme makeover! When the bus pulled away from the front of his spread, there stood bigger barns filled to the rafters with new grain. Satisfied, at least for the moment, he said to himself, "Self, you have arrived. Take it easy. Prop up your feet. Eat, drink, and have a glorious time. You deserve it." This farmer talked to himself a lot; perhaps in his greed he had destroyed any other meaningful relationship and had no one else to talk to. But he seemed quite content with his own company. How sad!

> I believe the Judean farmers of the first century were near to the heart of Jesus.

Up to this point in the parable, the crowd had followed every move; that's when Jesus threw them a curveball. Instead of the conclusion "and the farmer lived happily ever after," tragedy struck. You can almost hear the crowd gasp as Jesus called the farmer a *fool*. Just when the clever entrepreneur reached the point where he could relax and enjoy the fruits of his labor—surprise! *He died.* And everything he so desperately wanted was left behind for someone else to enjoy. The crowd didn't see *that* one coming. Do we ever?

The State of the Vineyard

Of all the parables generated by life on the farm, none has a more unexpected conclusion than the one this chapter explores. The setting is a different kind of farm—a vineyard (Matthew 20:1-16). With clusters of ripe grapes tugging at the weary vines, the owner of the vineyard headed into town early one morning to hire temporary help. Some work habits have changed little through the centuries. At harvesttime in America's southwest, migrant workers show up in well-trafficked spots every morning, just hoping to be hired by a farmer with a crop to pick.

In Judea at the time of Christ, the workday usually began at 6:00 AM and concluded at 6:00 PM. The parable's landowner made his hires from among the available workers; then he negotiated payment for the day. They settled on a denarius, the customary daily wage for an unskilled laborer or common soldier of the time. Minted by the Roman government, the denarius usually bore the emperor's image and contained one-tenth troy ounce of silver.[1]

Around 9:00 AM the owner returned to town to hire more workers. The job was bigger than he anticipated, and the first crew hired wouldn't even make a dent in the harvest. They desperately needed more help. With this second hire there was no wage negotiation; the farmer simply promised to pay "whatever is right." The workers were grateful for a job offer; they didn't argue. Back to town at noon and again at three o'clock the owner hired even more farmhands. Finally, with daylight waning and only sixty minutes of work time remaining, the opportunistic owner hired the last of the workers. Evidently, they had waited all day hoping against hope that someone would give them a job. Can you imagine the wave of relief that washed over these eleventh-hour hires? They would not go home empty-handed after all. I'm confident they had little expectation for very much pay, but if you can't have the whole loaf of bread, a slice is better than nothing.

So far, so good—nothing too surprising yet. As the laborers filtered in from the vineyard, however, the story took an unexpected turn. The workers lined up to receive their wages—seniority would normally rule the day. The farmer, however, instructed his foreman to pay the men beginning with the *last* ones hired. That certainly wouldn't be customary; some might even find it insulting. The foreman then gave a denarius to each of the eleventh-hour hires. Whoa! I suspect the early-morning crew could hardly suppress their grins. *If those guys got what was promised to us, then how much more are we getting?* No doubt these weary workers mentally began spending their anticipated bonuses as the foreman moved down the line to the 3:00 hires. Their smiles quickly faded, however, as the 3:00, then 12:00, and even 9:00 crews all got the same silver denarius.

Finally, those who had worked a full twelve-hour shift received their denarii. What they had so eagerly agreed to at 6:00 AM had become an insult at 6:00 PM. They were hot under the tunic! How dare the owner treat them so unjustly?

Lest Jesus' listeners were puzzled by this surprising development; more likely they were frustrated or even angry. Who was this businessman farmer, and how could he be so unfair? Surely Jesus paused to let this surprising element sink in before he continued. The early-morning crew grumbled at the owner's ethics and offered their best defense with a taste of whine. "These men who were hired last worked only one hour, and you have made them equal to us who have borne the burden of the work and the heat of the day" (v. 12). But the logic of the owner's response was irrefutable:

- Did you get what I promised to pay you? *Well . . . yes.*
- It's my money and I can spend or give it as I want, right? *Well . . . yes, you can.*
- Are you envious, and angry at my generosity? *Well . . . I shouldn't be angry at generosity, but yes, I suppose I am.*

The crowd was still mulling over the seeming injustice of the whole ordeal when Jesus hit them with the punchline—*the last will be first, and the first will be last.*

Willing Workers

Every time I read this surprising story, I struggle with its implication. My American perspective of justice is greatly offended by this inverted tale. If fair pay for a job done is the heart of this parable, then this story does reek of injustice. I empathize with those early-morning hires, don't you? How is it right to treat everyone equally?

> Can you imagine the wave of relief that washed over these eleventh-hour hires? They would not go home empty-handed after all.

But before you plan to make a poster and picket this parable, take a closer look at the theme. Jesus wasn't talking about fairness in this story. His focus wasn't the vineyard. It makes no difference whether this farm was the premier vineyard of the region or just an ordinary family-run business. It doesn't matter whether this harvest was a bumper crop or an average yield. The vineyard was simply the setting, and it represents the world.

Jesus' parable also wasn't focused on the quality of labor. We don't really know much about these migrant workers. Jesus mentions nothing about skill levels or previous experience. We don't know if some insisted on breaks throughout the day while others labored on tirelessly. Nothing is said about their work ethic. The parable does not even address the quality of work accomplished. This we do know—in the arena of availability, they all appeared equal. Each worker, regardless of the hour stamped on his time card, seemed as willing to work as those hired earlier.

> Perhaps they dawdled away the best hours of the day sipping a double caramel mocha Frappuccino at the marketplace coffee shop.

When the owner of the vineyard returned to the marketplace at 5:00 PM, he seemed startled and a bit incredulous to find willing workers still waiting. "Why have you been standing here all day long doing nothing?" he inquired. "Because no one has hired us," they answered (vv. 6, 7). At a glance some might conclude that these eleventh-hour laborers appeared lazy. Perhaps they slept late and missed the first wave. Perhaps they dawdled away the best hours of the day sipping a double caramel mocha Frappuccino at the marketplace coffee shop. Maybe they were too busy updating their Facebook pages to get out the door at the crack of dawn. Such idleness would not have been rewarded with a job. We recoil at lazy; I suspect every state in the Union jokes about their less-than-energetic state highway employees. How many highway workers does it take to fill a pothole? Ten—two to direct traffic, two to sit in the truck, three to supervise while leaning on their shovels, two to study the map, and one to fill the hole. In all fairness to the many hardworking highway crews, lethargic and uninspiring workers can be found in almost any profession.

These laborers in the parable, however, were not lazy. They simply lacked an opportunity to work. I admire their tenacity. They could have given up early and gone back home in defeat, but they didn't. And their persistence and patience paid off big time.

I know people who feel they have no opportunity to make a difference. In certain cases the opportunities are there; they just never see them. Others, however, wait a long while for that special opportunity to come along. On the Judean motherhood survey form, Elizabeth had checked the box marked *failure*. Far beyond the childbearing age, she was resigned to the fact that she would never give her husband, Zechariah, a son. But nine months after her priestly (and surprisingly speechless) husband was visited by an angel, Elizabeth gave birth to a healthy baby they named John. The son of Elizabeth's golden years grew up to be a mighty preacher of repentance. Those he baptized he pointed to the coming Savior. Of John, Jesus remarked, "I tell you the truth: Among those born of women there has not risen anyone greater than John the Baptist" (Matthew 11:11).

Don't give up if you think life has overlooked you in the distribution of opportunities. God isn't finished with you yet. Your prospects to leave your mark on history may not come until . . . well, the eleventh hour. So don't quit; be willing to serve. Make yourself available to God and keep your eyes wide open. God rewards such patient perseverance.

How Much Is Enough?

May I share another subplot lesson with you? For all that these vineyard workers had in common, there is at least one distinction among them. The early-morning hires who complained about the pay were the only ones who had no right to object. You see, the first group hired was the last group to have a negotiated wage. They knew what they would receive at day's end, while the other groups employed throughout the day were merely told they would be paid *whatever is right*. Of all the vineyard workers, those who knew the exact amount that the contract stipulated should have been satisfied. It wasn't until the latecomers received the same pay that they became indignant. Contentment is *so* fleeting.

Why are we so seldom satisfied? Legend has it that the industrial tycoon John D. Rockefeller was once asked, "How much money is enough?" To which he supposedly replied, "Just a little more."[2] I don't know if the story is true, but the answer certainly is. We never quite have enough.

Russian novelist Leo Tolstoy asked a similar question in his short story *How Much Land Does a Man Need?*[3] The young farmer Pahom overheard his wife defending their meager rural lifestyle to her sister who lived well in the city. Pahom winced with guilt that he could not provide better and thought to himself, *If I had plenty of land, I shouldn't fear the Devil himself.* As time went on Pahom worked hard and acquired a small plot of land, then a few more acres, then a whole farm. It was never enough. Eventually, he learned from a traveling salesman that tillable ground was cheap and available far away in the land of the Bashkirs. Leaving his family behind, he journeyed to the Bashkir territory and inquired of the Chief how he might purchase a farm. The Chief explained that his ground was sold by the day; for a thousand rubles Pahom could own all the land he could circumvent on foot between dawn and dusk. If, however, he did not return to the starting point before sundown, he forfeited his money and would receive nothing in return.

> We are a clear reflection of our Father when we share what we have been given.

With eyes as big as the prairie before him, Pahom began his trek early the next morning. Every step represented more land on his deed, so he pushed himself. Greed became a driving force as he picked up his pace. By mid-afternoon he was exhausted and much too far away from the starting point. He made his final turn and began to race against the fading daylight. As the sun started encroaching upon the horizon, he could hardly put one foot in front of the other, but he kept going. In the distance the Bashkirs started cheering him on; he stumbled forward and, just as the sun surrendered its last golden ray, he collapsed at the starting point. He made it! A cheer went up but Pahom did not rise. He was dead. How much land does a man need? A space about six feet long, three feet wide, and six feet deep.

Greed, that excessive desire to acquire more than a person needs or deserves, always destroys. The financial Ponzi scheme of Bernie Madoff is a prime example of greed's ruinous nature. Madoff spent a lifetime scamming people out of their wealth with the promise of healthy returns on their investments. Convicted and sentenced to 150 years in prison, he will most likely die in a two-person, nine-foot by twelve-foot cell—his half only slightly larger than a grave. For want of more, many investors placed all their eggs in Bernie's illusory basket and lost their life savings. Everyone suffers when greed is the driving force. Proverbs 28:25 says, "A greedy man stirs up dissension, but he who trusts in the LORD will prosper."

Grateful for Generosity

In contrast to such greed, Jesus wanted his listeners to grasp one truly significant point: God (the owner of the vineyard) is a *generous* God. He can be as generous as he wants to be, because he is the owner of all.

Generosity is such a winsome virtue. We like generous people. Those who engage in philanthropic ventures are always held in high esteem. But there are at least three other benefits to being generous with others.

1. *Generosity encourages.* We have all been cheered by another's unexpected gifts. Have you ever eaten at a restaurant when someone else picked up the tab? Free food usually tastes better, doesn't it?

2. *Generosity heals.* Dr. Karl Menninger wrote, "Money-giving is a good criterion of a person's mental health. Generous people are rarely mentally ill people."[4] I would suggest that generosity is also a barometer of spiritual health. "The righteous give generously" (Psalm 37:21). We are a clear reflection of our Father when we share what we have been given.

3. *Generosity surprises.* It's the unanticipated word of praise; the unexpected offer from a neighbor to share his time to help with your backyard project; the unforeseen check that shows up in your mailbox because an acquaintance wants to do something nice for you. Generosity always surprises.

Even more surprising, however, is when generosity is ignored. Who could be so callous? *We all can be.* When generosity is extended to us, etiquette demands a proper expression of thanks. How often do we take for granted, overlook, or flat out ignore all that the heavenly Father generously does for us? How often do we even fail to offer a simple prayer of thanks?

When Jesus told this surprising story about God's generosity, he was hoping for a spirit of gratitude in response. Like many people today and the itinerant farmhands in his parable, the members of Jesus' audience lived hand to mouth (see Leviticus 19:13 and Deuteronomy 24:15). Not many had burgeoning bank accounts at First National of Judea; it was a day-to-day existence. Some may have even been eleventh-hour hires at a point in their lives, but without experiencing such generosity. Unlike human landowners, the God of Heaven is not greedy, but generous in giving to all he loves.

After thirty-five years of preaching, I have been surprised by this parable in a way I never anticipated. Not long ago I sat down with Kenny Ooley to talk about his relationship with the Lord. Like so many, Kenny had put off a spiritual decision that he knew deep down he truly wanted to make. He didn't struggle with his faith; he struggled with his past. How could a perfect God love and forgive him for a lifetime of lousy choices? Could God be that generous? Could forgiveness extend that far? After all, he had wasted a lifetime without the Savior. With his sixty-second birthday just around the corner, he was convinced his best years were behind him. He expressed shame about being a Johnny-come-lately to the kingdom. "It isn't fair to sneak in at the eleventh hour and give God the leftovers."

Sound familiar? We always want to make it about us. *I* have been too bad. *I* have nothing to offer God. *I* don't deserve to be forgiven. True statements all. But therein lies our problem—it's not about us; it's about God. It's not about the farmhands; it's about the farmer. It's not about the fruit pickers; it's about the vineyard owner. It's his gift to give, and he can give it to whomever he desires.

Kenny and I talked for quite a while about God's generosity. He was afraid that if I baptized him he would somehow mess that up too. I reminded him that our goodness (or badness, for that matter) was not the determining factor. The Savior is good enough and generously invites us to serve in his vineyard regardless of the daylight left.

We prayed and I urged Kenny not to wait. A few days later he called and said, "I'm ready." He asked me to baptize him that Thursday afternoon, and I readily agreed. With a handful of close friends joining him, he and I stood in the baptistery. I heard him confess Jesus Christ as Lord with heartfelt passion. I lowered him into the water, and when he emerged, the weathered lines of his face gave way to a joy and peace like he had never known before.

> The Savior is good enough and generously invites us to serve in his vineyard regardless of the daylight left.

The following morning Kenny entered the hospital for what was to be a serious but routine surgical procedure. The result, however, was anything but routine. After a week-long battle Kenny's heart finally gave out and he went *home*. We buried him on his sixty-second birthday, but what a birthday celebration he must have been enjoying!

At his funeral one of Kenny's close friends read this very parable about the farmer and his vineyard. Never had that story seemed more relevant. I was no longer wrestling with the apparent wage inequity; I was at that moment celebrating God's generosity.

I think I've finally discovered my real issue with this passage through the years. You see, I'm one of those 6:00 AM workers. My name was on the cradle roll at church. At age twelve, on Easter Sunday 1967, I accepted Christ as my Savior and was baptized. I started preaching before finishing college. I've celebrated dozens of weddings, preached scores of funerals, and endured hundreds of meetings . . . ugh!

Maybe, just maybe . . . deep down . . . I didn't think it fair that on one's first time at bat, he could slide into the kingdom's home plate at the last moment and be called safe. After all, I've been running the bases faithfully for years. It just didn't feel right; that is, until Kenny. I thought I had been helping him spiritually, but all along he was helping *me* understand the God of the harvest better. I shouldn't be surprised at how God works—but

I always am. I will be forever grateful that God's generosity is distributed on his terms, not mine. And I will be forever grateful that we will share Heaven with Kenny Ooley and every other eleventh-hour worker in God's vineyard. The parable's punchline is now more relevant than ever; among those who had prayed for his salvation, Kenny was last to acknowledge the Savior but first to see his face!

I wish I owned a couple of those ancient Roman silver coins. One denarius I would have placed in Kenny's hand before the casket was closed—appropriate for an eleventh-hour hire. The other denarius I would keep in my pocket as a constant reminder to me—an early-morning hire—to be forever grateful that I serve a generous Lord!

1. The parable's vineyard was filled with willing workers. What are some characteristics of a willing worker in the Lord's church today? Some who serve aren't so willing. Does one's attitude matter to God, and if so, how?

2. How much is enough? Rockefeller may have been right—*just a little more*. Too often we want that car, house, or dream vacation that's just beyond our reach. Why is contentment so fleeting? List some ways you can improve your level of contentment.

3. "Generosity is such a winsome virtue. We like generous people. Those who engage in philanthropic ventures are always held in high esteem." List the benefits of being generous.

Didn't See That Coming
For individual or group study

4. God's generosity is unfathomable. How can we emulate his attitude? What qualities foster a generous spirit?

5. "It's not about us; it's about God. . . . It's his gift to give, and he can give it to whomever he desires." Have you ever wondered at God's generous gifts to others? When you see someone else receiving a blessing, which of these feelings is stronger in you—thankfulness for our generous God or envy of the receiver of the gifts? Why?

> Compassion is the sometimes fatal capacity for feeling what it is like to live inside somebody else's skin. It is the knowledge that there can never really be any peace and joy for me until there is peace and joy finally for you too.
> —Frederick Buechner, *Wishful Thinking*

It happened during the last week of April 2010, in Queens, New York. Hugo Tale-Yax donned the role of a Good Samaritan when a woman was attacked on 144th Street. Surveillance video shows the attacker trailing the lady as they walked under the protective scaffolding in front of a building, where he then assaulted her. Hugo came from the opposite direction and confronted the attacker. The grainy video shows a scuffle, but little else is visible. Both the assailant and the woman fled in opposite directions, but Hugo collapsed from multiple stab wounds. What happened next is the real tragedy. Nearly twenty-five people sauntered by, apparently indifferent to the bleeding man on the sidewalk. A couple of pedestrians paused to gawk, one physically shook him, one even took a picture with his cell phone—but none tried to help. Firefighters, responding to another 911 call, found his body eighty minutes after the attack.[1]

Be Compassionate
The parable of the roadside rescue
Luke 10:25-37

2

One has to wonder, had the first person on the scene demonstrated enough compassion to stay with the man and call 911, perhaps Hugo would have lived. Of this I am certain: in the absence of compassion, the man died. Ironic, isn't it? What the Good Samaritan needed was another Good Samaritan. Such characters, however, seem to be in short supply.

A Simple Question

The parable we know as that of the Good Samaritan tells of fearless and unconditional compassion. Not surprisingly then, this story is a close second to that of the Prodigal Son on my list of all-time favorite parables of Jesus. However, at the time Jesus first told it, it was anything but popular.

The twists and turns of the story are as winding as the road between Jerusalem and Jericho, where the main event occurred. But before exploring the actual parable, let's look at the context in which it was heard. Jesus told the story to illustrate his point—a point made during a battle of words over the subject of compassion. It all started with a not-so-innocent inquiry.

One day, an expert in the Law of Moses approached Jesus with a question—a question designed to test Jesus. The expert was more interested in traps than truth. After all, what could an expert possibly learn from this unorthodox Galilean preacher? "'Teacher,' he asked, 'what must I do to inherit eternal life?' 'What is written in the Law?' he replied. 'How do you read it?'" (Luke 10:25, 26). Turning the question back to the student, rather than simply giving an answer, was a common rabbinical approach. Jesus was saying, "You're the scholar, the expert—you tell me."

Experts are always ready and willing to state their position on any matter. The scholar answered Jesus by quoting from the Shema, from Deuteronomy 6:4, 5: "Hear, O Israel: The LORD our God, the LORD is one. Love the LORD your God with all your heart and with all your soul and with all your strength." Or to put it simply, love God with everything you are. But the man didn't stop with the obvious; he added a line from Leviticus 19:18, "Love your neighbor as yourself."

It is not clear whether the scholar was simply repeating what he had been taught, or if indeed he understood the powerful truth that loving one's neighbor *is* also a way of loving God. The two are difficult to separate. On another occasion when Jesus was questioned about the greatest commandment, he quickly pointed out that the Law and the Prophets rested on this very premise—love God, love others.

> ## It all started with a not-so-innocent inquiry.

I suspect Jesus smiled when he replied, "You have answered correctly." But before the man could bask in the warmth of this praise, Jesus added this postscript, "Do this and you will live." That must have stung! This biblical scholar undoubtedly believed he was already doing these things. But Jesus saw right past his pious façade. *Practice what you preach, Mr. Expert.* It was an embarrassing moment; no doubt the respected character desperately wanted to maintain his intellectual standing in the eyes of the crowd. Our resident scholar began to sweat; his plan unraveled as the whole conversation became *inverted*. As Jesus turned the tables on him, the scholar took a defensive stance. Trying to redeem his public image, he fired back, "And who is my neighbor?"

What Happened at Bloody Pass

Jesus siezed this opportunity. In the Greek, Luke 10:30 opens with the word *hupolabon*, which the *NIV* leaves untranslated. It means that Jesus "took up" the challenge laid down by this scholar; he jumped at the chance to drive home his point.[2] I almost feel sorry for the guy at this point in the conversation . . . almost. But in truth he got what was coming to him. He should have stopped while he was still behind, but he blindly pushed ahead. (It's never wise to go toe to toe with the author of the words in question.)

I envision the crowd being really into the conversation at this point. Perhaps some couldn't wait to see the smug, uppity know-it-all put in his place. But it's just as likely there were many who were hanging on every word, waiting for this so-called teacher to miss a step. Jesus then began one of his most poignant parables.

A man was going down from Jerusalem to Jericho. . . . I grew up in southern Indiana, and whenever someone spoke of "going down," that meant they were headed south toward Kentucky. If they were "going up," they were taking a trip north, probably to Indianapolis. "Going over" was either east or west; at that point you had to be good in geography to figure it out.

When reading this parable, one must not think like a Hoosier. Going down literally means going down. The trip from Jerusalem to Jericho was treacherous. The elevation dropped nearly 3,300 feet, as the road snaked its way seventeen miles to the town of Joshua's military fame.

> Once again, he heard more steps, another gasp, and then . . . eyes bent down to meet his.

No one traveled this road casually—no picnic tables or roadside rest areas existed along this route. And from Joshua's day this trek had a nickname; it was called Bloody Pass. Sounds like a sequel to *Gladiator*, doesn't it? Inhabited by robbers and roadside terrorists, the path earned its name. Anyone foolish enough to travel it alone deserved what he got. Enter our friend going down to Jericho. He was just an ordinary Joe—but the inevitable happened. Thugs and thieves poured out of their hiding places and attacked, giving *road rage* a whole new meaning. They plundered ol' Joe and left him bloody, beaten, and near death.

The man needed help—desperately. He knew he could not survive long in his condition without assistance. Every little sound startled him as it echoed off the craggy heights. The lengthening shadows along the narrow, stony path taunted him as he peered out through swollen eyes to catch a glimpse of any roadside rescuer. Suddenly, he heard footsteps; brisk at first but slowing as they neared. He couldn't lift his head to make eye contact, but he could reason from the robe's fringe that it was a temple priest. Hallelujah! Help had arrived.

Silence. Before he could speak, the feet stepped back and then hurried on more briskly than before.

Growing weaker with every passing minute, he wondered if there would be others. His ears, keen to his surroundings, picked up another sound. Was that humming? No, it was whistling. It sounded like one of those newfangled temple choruses he had heard while worshipping in Jerusalem. Probably not a priest, but maybe a worship assistant—a Levite. The whistling stopped; the Levite gasped. But before Joe could utter a sound, the Levite bolted from the scene as quickly as if someone had just entered the temple courts eating a pork tenderloin sandwich.

The temperature fell and with it, the victim's hopes. Worries swirled around in his aching head. What a miserable way to die, stuck in the shadows on Bloody Pass with no one to help get him home. Would his family ever know the truth about what had happened? Would his wife and children have to glean from the corners of other farmers' fields because they had no one to provide for them? Would there be rumors that he had abandoned his family to run off with some Jezebel floozy from Jerusalem? The haunting visions became even more desperate as his body grew weaker.

Once again, he heard steps, another gasp, and then . . . eyes bent down to meet his. The greeting was spoken with kindness, but the accent was unmistakably Samaritan.

It's all over now, he thought. *If only the priest or Levite had stopped, I might have had a fighting chance.* But at this point he was too weak to resist. Maybe if the Samaritan would just push him over the edge of the nearby cliff, the end would come quickly. He felt strong arms reach under his head and legs. He tensed and began to pray softly, "God of Abraham, Isaac, and Jacob . . ." but his body was not moved in the direction of the cliff. Rather, he was carried back into the sunlight. Gently the Samaritan placed him in the middle of the road; the heat from the late afternoon sun felt good on his cool body. Could it be that this disgrace of a man—if you could call him a man—was actually trying to help him?

He felt the sting of wine poured into his open wounds; the soothing warmth of olive oil followed the sting. The Samaritan tore off part of his robe and made crude bandages for the worst of his cuts, and then, with an oil-soaked cloth, he gently wiped the matted blood from the victim's face.

Once again Joe was lifted from the ground, then placed on the Samaritan's donkey. As the three of them ambled down the road, the rhythmic clomping of the donkey's hooves assured Joe that his deliverance had come—from the most unlikely roadside rescuer.

The inn at the end of the journey was like a haven in the midst of a storm. The weary and wounded traveler fell into a deep sleep. When he finally awoke he discovered that the Samaritan had not only paid the lodging expense but had also promised the innkeeper to pay whatever additional costs might be incurred until ol' Joe was well enough to go home.

Jesus may have paused to let the story sink in, and then posed this question, "Which of these three do you think was a neighbor to the man who fell into the hands of robbers?" (v. 36). I'm confident that at this point the scholar wished he had never even seen Jesus. There was no way to avoid answering. The crowd watched and waited. He couldn't bring himself to utter the word *Samaritan*, so the expert in the Law replied, "The one who had mercy on him." Jesus told him, "Go and do likewise" (v. 37).

It's How, Not Who

I realize the danger in making more of a parable than Jesus intended, but this story is rich in application. The heart of the issue wasn't the scholar's question, but the Savior's. It's not about the *who*; it's about the *how*. Technically, anyone in need is my neighbor. So how will I demonstrate the compassion of Christ when confronted with such desperate need?

We love this story! It's filled with a sense of adventure and intrigue, unexpected responses, good guys versus bad guys, and a happy ending. We also love it because it isn't so personal—we don't have issues with Samaritans. Most of us have never even met a Samaritan. Jesus' audience, however, certainly had! This story wasn't called the Parable of the Good Samaritan when Jesus first told it—in the minds of his Jewish audience there was no such thing. Those in attendance at the parable's premier weren't oohing and aahing with delight; they were squirming in their seats. Jesus pushed his listeners way out of their comfort zones with this inverted story; even his disciples were uncomfortable.

Let me suggest some evidence. As powerful as this story has been through the last twenty centuries, Luke is the only Gospel writer to include it in his narrative. It is incredible to note that neither Matthew nor Mark record any encounter with a Samaritan during the entire ministry of Jesus. And John mentions only one, the woman at the well (John 4). But Luke writes about three separate encounters. Why did Luke include these Samaritan stories when no other writer did? Luke wasn't a Jew. As a Gentile physician, Luke felt no bias or prejudice for the Samaritans. He had no dog in that fight.

Real Neighbors

Interestingly, the Jews and Samaritans *were* indeed neighbors. Samaria was sandwiched between Judea in the south and Galilee in the north. The quickest way from one to the other was straight through Samaria, but the hatred between the two races was so intense that a devout Jew would take the long way around, crossing to the east side of the Jordan and traveling through Perea and the Decapolis. Though the trip was considerably longer, it was worth it to avoid contact with any Samaritan.

Why such hatred? The nation of Judah viewed them as spiritual half-breeds—half Jew and half Gentile. The seed of Abraham had been compromised through intermarriage; the richness of God's Word had been diluted by idolatry. Hatred between the two groups only intensified as the years passed by. The feud between the Hatfields and McCoys looks like a Sunday school picnic compared to the animosity between the Jews and Samaritans.

> How will I demonstrate the compassion of Christ when confronted with such desperate need?

Jesus was determined to prove that the compassion of God is greater than any prejudice. To demonstrate his point he changed the life of a Samaritan divorcee at a well, healed a Samaritan leper in a border town, and cast the starring role in his parable to a Samaritan roadside rescuer. It's no wonder this story met with such a cool reception.

There is no room in God's kingdom for bias or prejudice. One color is not more desirable than another. One race is not more loved by God, nor more needed in the church, nor more anticipated in Heaven. All of us fit into one simple category—lost! It makes no difference whether you are male or female, rich or poor, formally educated or experientially educated, handsome or homely, popular or unpopular, liberal or conservative, red, yellow, black, or white—in this world, we are all lost without a Savior. In the church we are all one because of his grace. In a sense we are all neighbors because of a shared need.

Had Jesus told the story first in our culture and generation, it is certain he would not have chosen a Samaritan as the hero. What roadside rescuer would make you squirm? a drug addict? a Hell's Angel biker? a homosexual? a member of the Taliban? the boss you can't stomach? the nosy busybody who lives next door? the geeky twit that everyone picks on in class? the homeless guy you cross the street to avoid? your arrogant coworker who can do everything just a little better than you? Visualize the person you detest most in this world saving you, and you'll understand how this parable affected Jesus' audience. And maybe we'll all better understand how it is intended to impact us.

Like the scholar, we have at times been guilty of the same divisive spirit. We view ourselves as rich in mercy when in reality our compassion lives at poverty levels. Compassion cannot flourish in the soil of divisive bias. Jesus called on his first-century followers to give up their hatred and to love the unlovable; he challenges us to do the same. And just remember this—each one of us is unlovable at some point and in some way!

The lesson on prejudice is certainly valuable, but it only serves to enhance the main point of the parable. More than anything, Jesus taught us how to demonstrate God's compassion.

Seeing with 20/20 Vision

I wear contact lenses. I wouldn't dare get behind the wheel of a car without them—you wouldn't want me to! Every morning I gently place them on my eyes and the world is instantly clear again. I can see 20/20.

Wouldn't it be great if we could purchase a set of spiritual contact lenses that would help us see clearly what we so often overlook? It's difficult to be compassionate when you can't see the need. When the Samaritan happened upon the brutalized traveler, he seemed blind to the fact that the man was Jewish. Nor did he pause to analyze how rescuing "the enemy" might come back to haunt him. Oblivious to all the potential problems, he did see one thing with 20/20 vision—the desperate need of a wounded human being. He acted on the need alone and applied every asset within his possession to saving the man's life. When it comes to exercising genuine compassion, a person's need should determine how we respond.

> It's difficult to be compassionate
> when you can't see the need.

Our vision gets clouded when we make our compassion conditional. Do we only help those with future potential? Does our compassion only reach out to those who can reach back when *we* hurt? While he bandaged his wounds, the Samaritan didn't scold the traveler for his carelessness. Meeting the need was far more critical than the what-a-stupid-thing-to-do sermon he could have preached. My experience is that I don't need someone to remind me of my stupidity; I am painfully aware of my mistakes. What we need is someone to help us in our misery and to care for us despite our dumb decisions. Compassion must not be conditional.

It's hard to explain, but unconditional compassion sometimes returns as a blessing. On a hot July evening in 1999, Penny Brown had the night off from her nursing job in intensive care.[3] The break from work that evening gave her the chance to attend her son's Little League game. During the game the eleven-year-old bat boy, Kevin Stephan, was accidentally struck in the chest with a bat and collapsed. As Kevin's terrified parents watched helplessly, Penny rushed onto the field and discovered that Kevin's heart had stopped. She pounded on his chest and began CPR. Amazingly, Kevin's heart responded and he survived. Perhaps that life-altering episode inspired him to learn first aid. In any case, Kevin received education in life-saving skills first as a Boy Scout and then as a junior firefighter.

Fast-forward a few years. Seventeen-year-old Kevin was working as a part-time dishwasher at the Hillview Restaurant in Depew, New York, when he noticed a woman choking. Drawing on his first-aid training, he administered the Heimlich maneuver, and "two quick thrusts later," the dislodged piece of meat flew out. Kevin's mom was eating lunch in the restaurant that day and recognized the lady—it was Penny Brown, the nurse who had saved her son's life nearly seven years earlier. Kevin's comment said it all: "It's like divine intervention." Indeed, compassion expressed often returns as God's reward.

> How many times has your plan to serve God prevented you from God's plan for you to serve?

Compassion Goes Above and Beyond

Comedic actor Peter Ustinov said, "Charity is more common than compassion. Charity is tax-deductible. Compassion is time consuming."[4] Pity looks for the easy way out or the path of least involvement. Genuine compassion always goes above and beyond what is expected. In the parable, the priest and the Levite obviously saw a need, but their fear or excuses trumped what little compassion they may have had. Some suggest that the priest and the Levite were concerned that helping the injured man would have made them ceremonially unclean, thus disqualifying them from serving at the temple. But the priest and Levite were not headed up to Jerusalem; they were going down toward Jericho. Their temple duties were over; their spiritual obligations had been fulfilled.

I think, given the reputation of that road, it's possible that both the priest and the Levite feared the situation might have been a setup or trap. We understand that fear. I'll be honest; I'm often reluctant to help in suspicious circumstances, like picking up a hitchhiker or stopping to aid a stranded motorist. I guess I've read too many tragic stories about people who stopped to help and instead of finding a victim, became the victim. It's easy to be critical of the priest and Levite, but I suspect we have all acted similarly.

Perhaps they were in a hurry to do something else for God. It is easy to rationalize that someone else will come along to help. How many times has your plan to serve God prevented you from God's plan for you to serve? If we are busy doing God's work in some unique capacity, we often justify not getting involved because we have a duty to do. If we stop to help, our spiritual jobs may not get done. If you need clarity just ask yourself, "Would Jesus travel on down the road to do something important for God or would he stop to meet the immediate need?" Let compassion lead you; let it take you above and beyond what is expected.

The Samaritan's response was indeed above and beyond; he not only empathized with the man, he administered first aid, provided transportation, and paid the bills for his complete recovery. Wow! That wasn't just going the second mile, he went the third and fourth miles as well. When we go above and beyond what anyone expects or imagines, people notice. Such actions of compassion speak louder than any lesson or sermon ever could!

Compassion Moves Us to Action

Here is one of those ironies of life. When it becomes our primary goal to satisfy our own desires at the expense of others' needs, we rarely experience a moment of contentment. On the other hand, when we invest our lives in others, we discover a deep sense of satisfaction. There are wounded lives on the rocky path all around you. Open your eyes; it's not difficult to find hurting people who need a compassionate *you*. They hurt because:

- they are all alone.
- they suffer with a devastating physical disease or condition.
- they struggle with dysfunction and distrust in their homes.
- they mourn the death of one they loved dearly in this world.
- they feel stressed because they can't meet their financial obligations.
- they are empty because they don't know the only one who can fill the spiritual void in their lives.

I'm an Indianapolis Colts fan. I tend to be one who cheers from my sofa instead of the stands—tickets to any NFL game are costly! With an average ticket price of $75 per game, how many people do you think would buy season tickets to watch their favorite team just stand on the field and huddle for sixty minutes? No special team players running back a kickoff, no shotgun formations, no running plays or deep field pass plays, no third-down conversions, no nothing—just a sixty-minute huddle in the middle of the field. Who wants to watch that? Nobody. We pay to see some tough-hitting, hard-fighting action. Move that ball down the field and score!

We in the church can huddle up and talk about compassion all we want, but who wants to watch that? We've talked about it enough; talk is cheap. It's time to get in the game. The world around us needs to see some action. Let compassion lead you down the field and into the end zone of changing lives through Christ's love.

There is more than one Bloody Pass on this rugged journey. Don't run away from the need—get personal! Don't hold back; start looking for specific ways to help someone else now. And pray as you travel through life that God will give you Good Samaritan eyes and a Good Samaritan heart.

1. Are you a good neighbor? Don't answer that yet; consider how your neighbors would answer that question if they were being honest about you. What would they say makes you neighborly? What would they identify as areas of needed improvement?

2. Would Jesus consider you a good neighbor? Why or why not?

3. "The heart of the issue wasn't the scholar's question, but the Savior's. It's not about the *who*; it's about the *how*." How should you be neighborly? By Jesus' definition, a neighbor isn't limited to the person next door, but is anyone in need. What can you do to better address the needs of those around you?

Didn't See That Coming
For individual or group study

4. "There is no room in God's kingdom for bias or prejudice. One color is not more desirable than another. One race is not more loved by God, nor more needed in the church, nor more antici-pated in Heaven. All of us fit into one simple category—lost!" Why do some people look down on those of other races or cultures or socio-economic status? What makes us so biased? What are some practical ways in which we can break down the walls of prejudice?

5. "It's difficult to be compassionate when you can't see the need." How does one develop a compassionate vision or mind-set? From your perspective, what can you do to go above and beyond in meeting a need? When you see a homeless man, a disabled child, or a struggling widow, are you moved enough to take action or do you remain indifferent? What steps can you take to become a real roadside rescuer?

The important thing to remember when it comes to forgiving is that forgiveness doesn't make the other person right; it makes you free.

—STORMIE OMARTIAN,
SEVEN PRAYERS THAT WILL CHANGE YOUR LIFE FOREVER

Something was on Peter's mind. You can sense it in what he asked and how he asked it. Jesus had just finished teaching on confronting one's offender. "If your brother sins against you, go and show him his fault" (Matthew 18:15). The lecture must have stirred up an unpleasant memory for the fisherman, so when Jesus finished, Peter asked, "Lord, how many times shall I forgive my brother when he sins against me? Up to seven times?" (v. 21).

I'm not sure whether Peter was looking for an answer or a pat on the back. He asked and answered his own question all in one breath, assuming he would be applauded for his magnanimous heart. Seven exceeded the accepted norm. Many rabbis in that day limited the opportunity for forgiveness to only three offenses—three strikes and you're out![1] Undoubtedly, Peter was familiar with such traditions, so he doubled the limit and

Be Forgiving
The parable of the shocking servant
Matthew 18:21-35

3

added one for good measure. Surely seven—a number of completeness—would please the Master. Imagine then his surprise when Jesus answered, "I tell you, not seven times, but seventy-seven times" (v. 22).

Peter was stunned; he didn't see *that* coming. Jesus took Peter's seven and added seventy. (Seventy being the result of multiplying two perfect numbers of completeness—seven and ten. However, this passage is also sometimes interpreted as seventy times seven, or 490.) While Peter stood there slack-jawed, running the math in his head, Jesus told this parable, in three acts.

Act One

"Therefore, the kingdom of heaven is like a king who wanted to settle accounts with his servants. As he began the settlement, a man who owed him ten thousand talents was brought to him. Since he was not able to pay, the master ordered that he and his wife and his children and all that he had be sold to repay the debt" (vv. 23-25). Nothing indicates whether the king in this parable was a Jew or Gentile, real or imaginary. That he was a king *is* important because only an autocratic monarch with vast resources could make such comprehensive decisions. The king sought to settle accounts with those in his employ. One of his servants was head over heels in debt.

> The man pleaded for time and patience. . . .
> He was on the brink of losing everything.

Being accustomed to the American dollar, it is difficult for me to make the transition to another monetary system. Whenever I visit another country, the currency often looks and feels like play money. For instance, when I exchanged a few American dollars in Belarus, I was given Belarusian bills valued at 20,000 rubles. I had never felt richer in my life, until I bought a bottle of water and it cost me 6,000 rubles. What a letdown!

In this parable we are dealing with the currency of talents. What's a talent? A talent was the largest monetary unit available at the time. It was also a measure of weight, being nearly ninety pounds of gold, silver, or bronze. We tend to gloss over this 10,000-talent debt; it's a big number, but we are accustomed to big numbers like this when we buy a car, pay tuition, or purchase a house. That's because we are still thinking dollars. However, when Jesus threw out this figure, it would have taken the disciples completely by surprise. I'm not sure they could have fathomed such an amount.

Let me try to put this into perspective. If we assume that a talent was indeed ninety pounds, then the servant's debt would have been equal to about 450 tons of gold or silver. Herod the Great received from his entire kingdom annual revenue of 900 talents. Being in debt 10,000 talents would have been almost inconceivable to the disciples. Based on a day laborer's wage, it would have taken 164,000 years to repay.[2] In our culture such a parallel would have the servant owing the king millions upon millions of dollars. Incredible! The king, responding with justice, decided to sell the man, his family, and their belongings to recoup a small portion of the debt. Even at that, the best value a slave would bring was five hundred days' wages, a mere drop in the bucket compared to his overwhelming debt.[3]

"The servant fell on his knees before him. 'Be patient with me,' he begged, 'and I will pay back everything'" (v. 26). The man pleaded for time and patience. In his mind's eye he visualized the tearful scene of his family being split up and auctioned off to a variety of high bidders, never to be together again. He was on the brink of losing everything. You can hear the desperation in his voice as he promised to pay back every last penny, but both he and the king knew it was a hollow promise. What happened next was totally unexpected.

"The servant's master took pity on him, canceled the debt and let him go" (v. 27).

Unbelievable! The king would have deserved our heartfelt admiration had he extended the payment deadline or garnished the servant's wages for the rest of his life, but no, the king canceled the *whole* debt. He just wiped the slate clean, he stamped the bill "Paid in Full," and he canceled the contract he had with Dog the Bounty Hunter for roughing up the servant a little. Can you imagine how the man must have felt? Oh, the freedom of the moment that inconceivable burden was lifted!

How could the king do something so incredible? The text says he "took pity on him," but that hardly does justice to the story. For us *pity* is buzzing down the car window at an intersection to give the guy with the cardboard sign a buck. The word used in verse 27, however, is the strongest word in the Greek language for compassion—*splagchnizesthai*—which literally translates as "being filled with compassion." It is the verb form of the noun for the inner body parts—heart, lungs, liver, intestines, etc. Have you ever had an experience in which a situation moved you so deeply that your throat felt choked off with a lump, your heart throbbed, and your gut ached as if you had taken a punch? As a result you were compelled to respond— you couldn't help yourself.[4] This word means to shift your brain into neutral (which is easy for many of us) and follow the lead of your heart. And with the exception of its appearance in three parables, this word is only used of Jesus in the New Testament.

You don't have to be a financial genius to understand that God was so moved by our incomprehensible debt of sin that he canceled what he knew we could never pay. He stamped our bill "Paid in Full" with the blood of Christ. Words cannot describe the relief that comes when one has been redeemed from sin's pawnshop. Our souls are released from being in hock; we are no longer spiritually bankrupt. Our deficit is offset by his matchless, compassionate grace. The bounty hunter of Hell can no longer collect on our accounts.

The message of this divine pity is such a powerful truth, and yet it is not the point of the parable. However, understanding this truth is vital to seeing the contrast found in the next few verses.

Act Two

"But when that servant went out, he found one of his fellow servants who owed him a hundred denarii. He grabbed him and began to choke him. 'Pay back what you owe me!' he demanded. "His fellow servant fell to his knees and begged him, 'Be patient with me, and I will pay you back'" (vv. 28, 29).

This was not necessarily a miniscule amount—one hundred days' wages—but with time and patience, it could have been repaid. What's more, in comparison to the debt forgiven by the king, this amount was paltry. It was nothing but chump change.

> He stamped our bill "Paid in Full" with the blood of Christ.

"But he refused. Instead, he went off and had the man thrown into prison until he could pay the debt" (v. 30).

Talk about inverted! How could one who had been forgiven so much be so utterly absurd and cruel? There are no words to describe such disregard.

Act Three

"When the other servants saw what had happened, they were greatly distressed and went and told their master everything that had happened. Then the master called the servant in. 'You wicked servant,' he said, 'I canceled all that debt of yours because you begged me to. Shouldn't you have had mercy on your fellow servant just as I had on you?' In anger his master turned him over to the jailers to be tortured, until he should pay back all he owed" (vv. 31-34).

The lesson is nearly impossible to miss.

"This is how my heavenly Father will treat each of you unless you forgive your brother from your heart" (v. 35).

Supposedly, the last words of the poet Heinrich Heine were, "God will forgive me. It's His profession."[5] I wouldn't be so brazen or flippant about God's mercy, but there is a sense in which forgiveness is God's business. God created it, was the first to grant it, and is the only one who has the right to demand it of us. God extended to us his merciful forgiveness and in turn declared that it is our job to forgive others as well. Extending mercy and forgiveness to others is not particularly easy; as a matter of fact, it's downright difficult. Honestly, I don't really like this parable and its lesson. It strikes too close to home for comfort. But like it or not, this truth is undeniable, and we are obligated to obey.

Forgiving with No Limits

Why did Jesus tell Peter he was obliged to forgive seventy-seven times—is there something significant about this number? Some see a correlation between the words of Lamech in Genesis and this expression of Jesus. "Lamech said to his wives, 'Adah and Zillah, listen to me; wives of Lamech, hear my words. I have killed a man for wounding me, a young man for injuring me. If Cain is avenged seven times, then Lamech seventy-seven times" (Genesis 4:23, 24).

Lamech was the great-great-great-grandson of Cain, who killed his brother Abel. Judging from his own admission it would seem that Lamech killed a young man for wounding him. Perhaps the death was the result of self-defense. However, this bit of morbid poetry seems to suggest a presumptuous arrogance about Lamech's own strength. It's as if he was capable of doing more to protect himself than God was able to do in protecting or avenging Cain. That alone is frightening, but the boastful poem also glorifies personal revenge.[6]

> Extending mercy and forgiveness to others is not particularly easy; as a matter of fact, it's downright difficult.

The desire for revenge is a common response to inflicted pain, grief, or embarrassment; it comes easily. No child has to be taught to hit back—it just happens. The challenge comes in teaching a child *not* to hit back. That goes against the natural grain. This response of Jesus to Peter also cut against the grain. "No, Peter; holding grudges or seeking revenge is never OK, not even after forgiving seven times." In some ways we have more in common with Lamech than with Peter. After all, we have concluded that life is a war zone. We must inflict more pain on the enemy if we intend to come out victorious. Consequently, it seems necessary to even the score, and then some.

In his book *Everybody's Normal Till You Get to Know Them*, John Ortberg tells of a classic moment of sweet revenge. Several years ago, while living in Boulder, Colorado, Dave Hagler was pulled over for driving too fast in the snow. He didn't want a ticket; he apologized for his driving, kindly pointed to his good record, and shared his concern over rising insurance costs. But the officer was not distracted from his task. He gave the ticket to Dave and told him that if he didn't like it, he could take it to court. When baseball season rolled around the following summer, Hagler was umpiring behind home plate. Wouldn't you know it, the police officer who had cited him earlier in the year walked to the plate. Both men recognized each other, so the officer spoke up and asked, "How did the thing with the ticket go?" Hagler simply said, "You'd better swing at everything."[7]

Admit it—you like that story, don't you? I do too. We want everything to even out, but unfortunately, it never will in this world. Revenge fails; it only creates an atmosphere of escalating retribution. Payback time will cost you more than you can afford. Disagree? Ask Samson someday if losing his two eyes at the hands of the Philistines was worth the taste of revenge. We call it *sweet* revenge, but it never is. Like artificial sweetener, it may taste sweet at first but it leaves a bitter aftertaste and neutralizes your ability to taste anything else.

Much of country music strums the themes of disappointment and resentment. The title of this song says it all: "While My John Deere Was Plowing the Field, Her Dear John was Plowing My Heart." When we've been hurt or angered by another, it's natural to want to strike back. Only God can pronounce the perfect judgment—but that doesn't keep us from trying. A harsh word, a cold shoulder, a steely glance, an exaggerated tale in the gossip club—all is done in an attempt to hurt the offender like we have been hurt. In the movies, when the bad guy gets it, do you find yourself muttering, "All right! He had it coming!" To a degree don't we all have it coming?

The apostle Paul said, "Do not take revenge, my friends, but leave room for God's wrath, for it is written: 'It is mine to avenge; I will repay,' says the Lord" (Romans 12:19). Here are a couple of thoughts to keep in mind when vengeance rears its ugly head in your soul.

Remember how much God has forgiven you.

God will never ask you to forgive someone more than you've already been forgiven by God. Hypothetically speaking (I know *you* wouldn't do this), what would happen if you exceeded the speed limit—and got caught—*every* day? In sixty years of driving you would accumulate nearly 22,000 traffic tickets. Wow! How long would it take before you had no driver's license or money enough to pay the fines? When would you be declared a menace on the highway? That's not going to happen, but what if you sinned in thought, word, or action only once a day? That would be a *really* good day for me. But even if every day were a really good day and we sinned only once each day, in a lifetime of seventy-five years we would stand guilty before God with a list of more than 27,000 transgressions against his law. That's way past the seventy-seven that troubled Peter. When you are tempted to hold a grudge, remember how many of your sins God has released.

Remember that God is in control.

When you've been hurt, the offender may have meant it for bad, but God can and will use it for good in your life. Consider Paul's words in Romans 8:28: "in all things God works for the good of those who love him, who have been called according to his purpose." The promise doesn't say that all things are good; we know that's not true. God promises that he can use anything in our lives to produce good results. That's the very thing Joseph said to his brothers when they returned to Egypt to buy more food.

Perhaps you remember Joseph's story. Seventeen-year-old Joseph was betrayed by his own family, sold into slavery by his hateful brothers, falsely accused of rape by the woman who tried to seduce him, thrown into prison by the jilted woman's husband, and forgotten by Pharaoh's cupbearer whom he had helped. He had no idea why his life had taken so many wrong turns—he had tried to do what was right. And yet he trusted God the whole time; he maintained a forgiving spirit. God knew exactly what was going on and had Joseph exactly where he wanted him.

In time God elevated Joseph to second-in-command in all of Egypt. Only Pharaoh himself was greater than him, and since Egypt was the most powerful nation in the world at the time, one could say that Joseph had arrived! His skillfully organized plan to save up grain in the years of abundance saved two nations—Egypt and Israel—when the seven-year famine swept through the land.

Now when his brothers came to Egypt to buy grain, they appeared before the vice pharaoh. But they did not realize who he was. After determining their repentant hearts and changed attitudes, Joseph revealed himself to his brothers. Imagine their terror, as they were convinced he would kill them—yet through his tears of joy, Joseph said, "You intended to harm me, but God intended it all for good. He brought me to this position so I could save the lives of many people" (Genesis 50:20, *NLT*).

Read and remember.

When Jesus dropped the numeric bomb of seventy-seven times (or 490), it was not intended to be taken literally. Jesus wasn't suggesting that on the seventy-eighth offense, Peter could punch the guy in the nose. It was merely to communicate that there are *no limits* to the number of times we should forgive.

The sentiment expressed in the parable is not unique to this one passage. Have you paid close attention to these words contained in the Lord's Prayer? "Forgive us our debts, as we also have forgiven our debtors" (Matthew 6:12). In Luke 6:37, Jesus told his listeners, "Forgive, and you will be forgiven." Paul wrote to the Colossian Christians, "Bear with each other and forgive whatever grievances you may have against one another. Forgive as the Lord forgave you" (3:13). He wrote much the same to the Ephesians. And on the cross when every breath mattered and words were uttered at great physical cost, Jesus spoke first with a prayer of forgiveness, "Father, forgive them, for they do not know what they are doing" (Luke 23:34). If the very Son of God could forgive those who crucified him, what offense have you suffered that you can justify *not* forgiving?

Remember—no limits.

Forgiving with No Lines

When human beings are under attack, we tend to take refuge behind a line—this line of defense can be anything from a company of soldiers stemming the tide of an encroaching enemy to a verbal barrage of argumentative words from our own mouths. Busy with protecting ourselves, we offer flimsy rationalizations for our lack of mercy: "You don't know how much I've been hurt;" "I just can't get past what they did to me;" "Every time I see him my stomach knots up;" "She won't even admit what she's done." We draw these lines of defense as if such explanations justify our failure to forgive. Let's be honest, most of us believe that though *we* deserve mercy, others are suspect.

> Nothing builds Christlike character faster
> than learning to forgive as he has forgiven you.

Forgiving others is one of the most difficult of Christian commands to carry out, but nothing builds Christlike character faster than learning to forgive as he has forgiven you. The problem is, we misunderstand forgiveness. It's not about letting someone off the hook or rationalizing away the offending deed to make it seem suddenly OK. It's not about becoming best friends with the offender or going out to eat with him or her weekly. The nature of forgiveness is more for us than for the other person. When you don't forgive, you bear the burden of bitterness, you stumble under the weight of a grudge, you smolder with a hot anger, and you become unpleasant to be around because your frustration makes you negative and cynical. The offender goes on his merry way, but you're the one who loses.

Stop drawing up lines of defense—there are no lines God can't see right through. Let me suggest three attitudes you can adopt in order to break down your barriers.

1. *Be understanding.* Seek first to understand before you seek to be understood. Give the offending person the benefit of the doubt, and you may discover that your hurt was unintentional.

2. *Be obedient.* Do what is right, not what feels good. If we base forgiveness on our emotions, we will never forgive. Make it an exercise of spiritual obedience, whether you feel like it or not. When it comes to forgiveness, your emotions are not reliable. Use your brain and be obedient.

3. *Be prayerful*—forgiveness comes through prayer. I'm not sure complete and genuine forgiveness is even possible apart from the strength God can impart. Ask the Lord to supply the feelings as you supply the obedience. At the right time, you might even offer to pray with the offender. It is really difficult to hold a grudge at the same time when you're holding another's hand in prayer.

No Liberty without Forgiving

There can be no liberty if we choose to hang onto liabilities. Forgiveness will set us free.

I met Florence Dace several years ago in Springfield, Illinois, when I was preaching a revival at the Southside Christian Church. She was one of the few who made it every night to pray with the church staff and me before the services began. There was something about this gracious, elderly lady that captivated me. Her prayers touched my heart and though quietly offered, were powerful in their sincerity. It wasn't until the end of the week that I learned her story. Since that time I cannot think of the subject of forgiveness without thinking of Florence Dace. I have never met a better model of Jesus' words. Let me tell you her story.

In the 1970s Florence's husband, Tom, worked as a local contractor in Springfield and was at the time remodeling an apartment. Tenant Frank Sherry lived in the apartment directly above the one where Tom was working. Strung out on drugs, Frank nearly went berserk from the noise of Tom's pounding and power tools. Finally, he could stand it no longer; he burst into the apartment below, picked up a claw hammer, and beat Tom Dace to the point of death. Tom died a few days later. The police wasted no time in apprehending Frank Sherry, who was subsequently convicted of murder and sentenced to do time.

Tom had faithfully served as an elder at Southside for years, but what Florence did following the trial defies human logic. Along with her preacher, Bob Green, Florence went to the jail to see Frank Sherry. That's not all. She spoke to him of her forgiveness and then proceeded to give the murderer her husband's Bible. She added that it was the only thing that could possibly save him. Sometime later Florence received word that as a result of reading Tom's Bible, Frank had become a Christian. That's when she started visiting him regularly. There in prison the widow taught the convict the Word of God. It was no surprise then, when Frank was eventually released, that he went into the ministry. Why? One petite woman with a giant faith and the compassion of the King demonstrated divine forgiveness.

> There in prison the widow taught the convict the Word of God.

Some years later Southside invited Frank to return and share his testimony. At the end of the service, Florence came forward and gave him a hug. I will never be able to preach a better sermon than that snapshot of mercy. Both Florence and Frank have since gone home to Heaven, but her story continues to inspire me and countless others. I knew that first night of the revival when we prayed together, there was something extraordinary about Florence Dace—only later did I discover that I had been in the presence of spiritual greatness! Such is the power of forgiveness.

1. Based on rabbinical teachings, Peter thought himself generous to offer forgiveness up to seven times. How do you respond to Jesus' dictate of unlimited forgiveness? Is that a reasonable expectation or too much to ask of a mere human heart? Why do you say that?

2. "We want everything to even out, but unfortunately, it never will in this world. Revenge fails; it only creates an atmosphere of escalating retribution." Have you ever been guilty of revenge? How did it feel? List some ways you can eliminate the bitterness that results from being wronged.

3. Is forgiveness necessary if the offender does not apologize or seek your forgiveness? Are you obligated to forgive someone who doesn't even know he or she has wronged you? Explain your reasoning. How is forgiveness unconditional, or is it?

Didn't See *That* Coming
For individual or group study

4. Think about a time when you were forgiven by someone else. How did receiving forgiveness change your behavior after that time? Now consider whether or not you have ever felt unforgiven by someone. How does the way we approach forgiveness shape our relationships with friends, family, or even strangers?

5. Do you see forgiveness as a strength or weakness? Explain your answer. When you forgive, who does it help more—the offender or you? Why?

Those who would avoid the despair of sinfulness by staying far from God find they have also missed the forgiving grace of God.

—Charles E. Wolfe

You Can't Go Home Again—published posthumously in 1940, this novel by Thomas Wolfe carries a title that is more familiar than the book itself. The story centers around an author, George Webber, who writes about his hometown, Libya Hill. Webber's book is an immediate success; it's celebrated everywhere . . . that is, everywhere except for Libya Hill. Smaller towns tend to be rather private. The community folks may know everyone else's business, but they certainly don't want their dirty laundry hung out where the whole world can see it. Webber didn't spare any details; he related all the sordid events of hometown lives, including members of his own family. Though George had anticipated being hailed as a hometown hero following the book's debut, instead of notes of praise his mailbox is filled with letters of scorn and outrage. With his pen, he had betrayed his hometown and the people he loved. In return, the community responded with anger and threats on his life. George determines never to return to Libya Hill; after all, you can't go home again.

Be Gracious

The parable of the warmest welcome

Luke 15:11-32

4

You can't go home again. Do you believe that? Have you burned all your bridges and severed every tie? As a culture we've come to accept Wolfe's premise as true more often than not. Didn't Thomas Wolfe *ever* read the fifteenth chapter of Luke? It tells an altogether different story about going home.

A Tale of Two Sons

"There was a man who had two sons . . ." (Luke 15:11). We didn't have any sons, but my wife and I raised two daughters who differed enough in appearance and personality that our pediatrician wanted to know if one was adopted. I don't know if the two sons in Luke 15 differed in looks, but they certainly differed in personality and character.

Isn't it amazing how no two of us are exactly alike? The complexity of our DNA is such that we stand alone throughout human history—each a one-of-a-kind model. I like the fact that we are so unique. There will never be another you . . . or me! What an amazing gift from the Father's creative genius. King David said it best: "I praise you because I am fearfully and wonderfully made; your works are wonderful, I know that full well" (Psalm 139:14).

"The younger one said to his father, 'Father, give me my share of the estate.' So he divided his property between them" (Luke 15:12). Undoubtedly, the father sensed the restlessness of his younger son as he complied with the request. The young man got his inheritance early; actually, both sons did. The inheritance was divided between the *two* of them. It's not clear if the younger son had any specific plans for the money at the time of his request, but it didn't take him long to devise a strategy for the days ahead or a rationalization for leaving home. The thoughts swirling around in his head might have been something like this: *Could anything be as lame as wasting my time on this out-of-the-way ranch? Stupid cows are always getting lost in the surrounding ravines or wandering onto our crabby neighbor's land. I'm tired of smelling like livestock; I'm tired of working shoulder to shoulder with a goody-two-shoes brother who never messes up; I'm tired of Dad always telling me what to do. I'm just not cut out to be a rancher—I'm outta here.* And with that the young man "set off for a distant country" (v. 13).

In our minds a distant country would likely require a trip to another continent. But Jesus' listeners would not have been so farsighted. Consider the following possibility. Later in his ministry Jerusalem ceased to be a safe place for Jesus as the Jewish religious leaders plotted his demise. Consequently, the Lord sought refuge on the east side of the Jordan River in an area identified as Perea.[1] It is here in Perea where Jesus likely told this parable.

> I don't know if the two sons in Luke 15 differed in looks, but they certainly differed in personality and character.

Just to the north of Perea was the region known as the Decapolis. In the Greek, *deca* means "ten"; *polis* is translated as "city." Ten Cities—Greek cities to be accurate, but all were under Roman domination and protection. During this period the Decapolis thrived. Exquisite temples for worship and bulging amphitheaters for entertainment dotted the landscape. The arts and literature flourished. Sporting events drew huge crowds. All of this was just a few miles up the road. Undoubtedly some of these structures would have been visible on a clear day. And I suspect that, in the cool of the evening, one could sit on the flat roof of his house and hear festive music and laughter as it wafted southward.[2] Pig farmers were numerous in the region too. Remember in Mark 5:13 when Jesus healed the demoniac in the Decapolis and the disenfranchised demons entered a pig herd that took a dive? Keep that image in mind because a pig farm plays a major role in this parable. And the region was also home to soldiers of the Roman tenth legion (6,000 soldiers). Charged with keeping the peace in and around Judea, the icon or symbol for this Roman legion was (are you ready for this?) a boar's head.[3] And you thought Washington, D.C., was the only place with this much pork!

I wonder if, when Jesus told this parable, he pointed north as he spoke of the younger son setting off for that distant country. Not so far away in miles, but far away in values. A little ways up the road was a whole new world of pork-eating Gentile idolaters, just waiting to filch his Jewish inheritance.

From Riches to Rags

"And there [he] squandered his wealth in wild living" (Luke 15:13). Did you ever squander anything? A tax refund perhaps? How about an opportunity? Maybe your education? *Squandered.* The word even sounds careless and wasteful, doesn't it? I have a mental image of this young man hunkered down over gaming tables, gambling away his money like he owned the mint. I can see him surrounded by pretty Greek girls who gushed over him so long as the money flowed as freely as the wine. Expensive clothes, rich and delectable food, lavish parties—*wild living.* An inheritance wouldn't last long in a distant country like the Decapolis.

The economy tanked about the same time his fortune dwindled away to nothing. A famine swept through the land like a band of ruthless raiders. Unemployment skyrocketed. No crops; no work. The few remaining jobs went to the locals, not to some foreigner whose pockets just came up empty. In exasperation, the young man took a menial job with a local farmer.

That in itself was bad enough, but the farmer put him to work feeding pigs. To us a pig is just an ordinary, albeit highly intelligent, farm animal. Thanks to the children's novel *Charlotte's Web* that introduces us to the amazing pig Wilbur, the comical Looney Tunes stuttering Porky Pig, and the oddly endearing movie about a sheepherding pig called *Babe,* we've come to appreciate the cute little oinkers. Feeding pigs is no big deal to the twenty-first-century, non-Orthodox Jewish mind. But when Jesus came to this part of the story, you could have heard the collective gasps and moans of his audience all the way up in the Decapolis. No word picture painted a better representation of desperation and ethical compromise than that of feeding pigs. In the Jewish mind, pigs seemed to epitomize everything unclean. Of all the land animals listed in the Law as unclean, the pig is singled out as both uneatable and *untouchable* (see Leviticus 11:7, 8; Deuteronomy 14:8).

It got worse. The young man who so recently had been the life of the party became desperate enough that he longed to eat the seed pods that the pigs had touched and rejected. Surely the mothers in the crowd were hiding their faces at the thought of their Jewish sons caught in such a dilemma. It was a scene that surprised everyone.

Aha Moment #1

"When he came to his senses . . ." (Luke 15:17). This was the first of several aha moments in the parable. Could there be a better description of true repentance? There in the mud, slop, and pig manure the younger son finally woke up. For the first time since leaving the ranch, he took an honest look at himself . . . and it wasn't pretty.

- He had abandoned the one place he could really call home.
- He had turned his back on the only ones who genuinely loved him for who he was, not for what he had.
- He had frittered away his entire inheritance and had absolutely nothing to show for it.
- He had scrounged up the most disgusting job imaginable and was glad to have it.
- He had less to eat than the pigs.

He'd had enough. He knew no one else was to blame for his current circumstance and no one else could turn it around. A change was needed—a drastic, humiliating, groveling kind of change. The choice was clear. He fed the pigs for the last time and set off for home.

Senseless Sin

Repentance—that change of mind that motivates a change of behavior—is not a hot topic of sermons or discussions these days. We love studies and messages that address our felt needs and current twenty-first-century challenges. Don't get me wrong; I love that style of message too. But I fear that in our heartfelt efforts to be culturally relevant, we have abandoned the relevant need for heartfelt repentance. Most preachers today would likely lose their pulpit privileges if every sermon focused on repentance, and yet John the Baptist spent his entire earthly ministry boldly proclaiming that one central theme. Jesus himself said, "Unless you repent, you too will all perish" (Luke 13:5).

It is so easy to be critical of this young man, but consider for a moment what pigs you are feeding. What wasteful, tempting issues are hogging your time, attention, and resources?

Perhaps you're bending the rules to get ahead in your career. You're determined to get to the top at any cost. You'll use anything or anyone along the way to accomplish your goal, and you don't care who gets hurt in the process. After all, the ends justify the means, right? Sadly, when you reach your destination you may be surprised to discover that you're not at the top, but all alone in the muddy sty. Before that happens, come to your senses.

Are you the person who, when your best friend gets a forty-six-inch flat-screen TV, has to buy a fifty-two-inch plasma 3-D TV with surround sound—even when you can't afford one? Do you always have more month at the end of your money? Does your checkbook squeal like a stuck pig every time you pay a bill? If you are eating so high on the hog that your debt would embarrass the U.S. Congress, then I've got news for you. One of these days you'll find yourself with empty pockets and an empty life in the land of financial famine. Before that happens, come to your senses.

> ## What wasteful, tempting issues are hogging your time, attention, and resources?

Does your marriage feel dull and uninspiring? Do you and your spouse work so hard to bring home the bacon that you neglect each other? Is the relational grass looking greener on the other side of the fence? If you're gazing at some other pretty face, thinking that all your troubles would be over if you could just be together, then I've got a farm report for you. Don't cast the pearls of faithfulness before swine. Make it your goal to put new life in your relationship; don't make a new relationship your life's goal. Destroy your home and family, and the stench will be worse than any pigpen. Before that happens, come to your senses.

"'How many of my father's hired men have food to spare, and here I am starving to death! I will set out and go back to my father and say to him: Father, I have sinned against heaven and against you. I am no longer worthy to be called your son; make me like one of your hired men.' So he got up and went to his father" (Luke 15:17-20). The home he'd so desperately wanted to escape now promised a way of escape from the misery of his life.

We seldom know what we have until we lose it. When the young man reflected on his former life, he discovered in his memory a picture of a father who had provided a wonderful example. There in the mud of the pigsty an image came to mind. It was the wonderful way his father treated the hired help. His dad had been more than gracious and kind to those in his employ. So the young man reasoned, given his father's kindness, he would go back home, openly admit his sin, then hire on as a ranch hand.

I never cease to be amazed at sin's stupidity. Pick up a newspaper on any given day and it will verify that truth. In March 2010, Connecticut resident Albert Bailey needed some extra cash and decided to rob an area bank.[4] Perhaps Albert suffers with a slight obsessive/compulsive disorder. Or maybe he reasoned that if call-ahead-waiting works for restaurants, then call-ahead-banking would work for a robbery. Giving the tellers a ten-minute lead to round up the loot, Albert and his sixteen-year-old sidekick entered the bank to a warm welcome by local police. Sgt. James Perez was quoted as saying the suspects were "not too bright."

Duh! Sin does that to a person. Repentance, on the other hand, results in wisdom. Look at the younger son's repentant conclusion: it's logical, sensible, and doable. It was the first smart action he took! When genuine repentance leads a person to embrace God's standards and principles, the end result is always a smart move. Wise up and leave the stupidity of sin far behind. Turn around and head for home.

Aha Moment #2

"But while he was still a long way off, his father saw him and was filled with compassion for him; he ran to his son, threw his arms around him and kissed him. The son said to him, 'Father, I have sinned against heaven and against you. I am no longer worthy to be called your son.' But the father said to his servants, 'Quick! Bring the best robe and put it on him. Put a ring on his finger and sandals on his feet. Bring the fattened calf and kill it. Let's have a feast and celebrate. For this son of mine was dead and is alive again; he was lost and is found.' So they began to celebrate" (Luke 15:20-24). This is the second aha moment in the story and an even bigger surprise than the pigpen scene. Confident that the father would exact a heavy penalty for such waste and sinful indulgence, the crowd anxiously waited through this part of the story for the other sandal to drop. It never did.

In all fairness to the crowd, parental logic often demands that for every hug there should be a wagging finger in the face. For every kiss there should be an I-told-you-so glare. A robe and a ring come with a price. There can be no party until the prodigal proves himself worthy again. Such is the just response of human logic. Such is the reaction of the typical parent.

But this father isn't the typical parent; he doesn't fit the mold. It's as if whatever had happened in the long months of his son's absence was inconsequential compared to his return. In the father's great joy, all was forgiven.

"Wait a minute," we object, "how can that be fair? There must be consequences for his actions. Such lack of discipline will result in an even more spoiled son." But there *were* consequences. The father would have noticed them immediately. By the time the son reached home, his remaining clothes were tattered and stained; they reeked from the stench of tending pigs. And what was left of his robe hung on a frame far gaunter than when he left home. Hunger peered through his weary eyes—his stomach was empty and so were his pockets. Indeed, there had been consequences to his choices. Still, it seems that old Dad let him off the hook far too easily, doesn't it?

Grace vs. Justice

We crave fairness. We want the scales of justice to balance. Unfortunately, the presence of sin guarantees otherwise. Innocent people sometimes suffer because of the evil choices of others. Show me a despot and I'll show you hordes of suffering people. It's not fair, but that's life in a broken world.

In the midst of our pain and anguish we cry out for impartiality, but is that what we truly need? The heartbeat of this parable isn't justice; it's a treasure far more valuable—grace. The word *grace* throughout the New Testament is the Greek word *charis* from which we derive such English words as *charisma* or *charm*. The word basically means "favor." Among the many definitions of grace, you may have heard these:

- God's unmerited favor
- A gift that makes glad
- An unearned eternity

Each definition is good and explores a slightly different facet of this priceless gem of God's salvation, but none of these provided the depth of understanding nor impacted my life so profoundly as the biblical principle I learned while a graduate student at Cincinnati Christian University. One day in Dr. Jack Cottrell's class, "The Doctrine of Grace," he introduced the concept of grace "as the opposite of law."[5] I knew, as Christians, we were no longer under the law nor were we saved through law keeping. I had certainly preached that being good enough wasn't good enough; that we are saved only by God's grace. But I had never heard the concept of grace being the actual opposite of the law.

All law systems work virtually the same whether physical, governmental, or moral. Dr. Cottrell went on to explain the tenets of law. *Keep the commandments (rules) and one escapes the penalty; break the commandments (rules) and one suffers the penalty.* That made perfect sense, although it did call to mind unpleasant memories of speed zones, police cruisers, and flashing red lights in my rearview mirror. I clearly understood the part about *break the law and suffer the penalty.* He continued by drawing the contrast with the tenets of grace. *Break the commandments and one escapes the penalty; keep the commandments and one suffers the penalty.*

Huh? How could that be? I'd always thought of God as being completely fair, but now I was confused. Hypothetically, if a person could actually keep the commandments perfectly, then why would he or she have to suffer? Perhaps Dr. Cottrell saw the puzzled look in my eye and knew if he gave me a little more rope, I would verbally hang myself. I did. I interrupted and asked, "How can that possibly be fair?"

He smiled (one of those professorial gotcha smiles) and agreed that it *wasn't* fair. But then, you see, grace itself isn't fair. He then proceeded to remind me that One had indeed kept the commandments perfectly, but by the rules of grace had to suffer the penalty. As a result, all the rest of us who have broken the commandments can now potentially escape the penalty.

Suddenly the incredible impact of what Jesus accomplished at the cross hit me like a ton of bricks. I had thought of grace in numerous ways, but never as *unfair*. For me, that single word *unfair* is the most profound description of grace. We claim we want divine justice in this world, but do we really? I don't want God to be fair to me; I just desperately need him to be gracious. When it comes to my salvation, don't give me justice; give me grace!

The father in this parable extended grace to his son. You might be thinking, *But hadn't his son wasted the inheritance?* Yes. *Hadn't he disgraced the family name?* Undoubtedly. *Well, then, shouldn't there be a penalty?* It depends; if you want the father to be perfectly fair, then yes. Justice demands a conditional acceptance. Junior must:

- relinquish all rights as a son.
- take up residence among the hired hands.
- buy his own clothes and food.
- have his wages garnished until the inheritance is recouped.

Conditional justice is what the younger son expected when he returned, but that would have made for a lousy story. What he received was unconditional love and grace.

We love this parable, but not because it's the story of a nameless father and his rebellious son. It's *our* story! In this parable Jesus pulled back the curtain of eternity and gave us a glimpse into the gracious heart of God our Father. Charles Dickens said of this parable, "It is the finest short story ever written."[6] That is true because of the hope inherent in God's grace.

I cling to this picture of the heavenly Father watching for us to come home. See him standing there at the end of the lane—craning his neck to catch any little movement in the distance, straining his ear for any hopeful sound of return. He never tires of watching and waiting. I take tremendous comfort from Peter's second letter, "The Lord is not slow in keeping his promise, as some understand slowness. He is patient with you, not wanting anyone to perish, but everyone to come to repentance" (2 Peter 3:9).

And when he finally sees us dragging our sin-weary souls up the road, he doesn't wait with an arm-crossed stance for us to reach him. No, he picks up the hem of his robe and joyfully runs to meet us.

In the Middle East of Jesus' day, normally, running was an act of indignity for a man.[7] God our Father, however, doesn't stand on etiquette; he dashes down the road because he can't wait to welcome us home. Overwhelming, isn't it? God, who spoke the universe into being, spun every galaxy into place, and knows every star by name, *runs* to welcome you home!

The father in the parable threw his arms around the son and covered him with kisses despite the grime and stench of a life wasted on sin and swine. A beautiful robe was fitted over a filthy body, a gold ring placed onto a grungy finger, clean sandals slipped onto once manure-encrusted feet. The contrast was startling and almost comical. Only the grace of God could be so oblivious to the tattered rags of our past.

And that's not all! The party planning committee went into full swing, killing the fattened calf for the welcome home celebration. The father spared no expense because the way he saw it, it was a miracle—a resurrection! "For this son of mine was dead and is alive again; he was lost and is found."

> I don't want God to be fair to me; I just desperately need him to be gracious.

A few years ago I had the privilege of spending some time in India with Central India Christian Mission. One evening Ajai Lall took us to visit a Hindu temple and monastery in a neighboring town during a religious festival. We walked through the temple as hundreds worshipped. I have never felt such an oppressive pall come over my soul. About that time our missions minister took a picture, and the crowd reacted . . . and I do mean *reacted*. I don't understand the Hindi tongue, but *angry* is the same in any language. We hurried out of the temple and into the monastery.

The young men (mostly teens) who lived in the monastery and were studying under the tutelage of their Hindu guru shared their beliefs by chanting for us what they were learning. I saw no joy in their faces; their eyes seemed hollow and empty of hope. When they finished, the Indian guru turned to me and asked about my faith. Surprise! I didn't see that coming in a Hindu house of worship. I shared the Parable of the Prodigal Son and explained that the God I serve, my heavenly Father, is a God of grace and offers forgiveness to those who will come to him in Christ. I hope the Lord will forgive me for editing his story just a bit—I left out the part about killing the fattened calf. We already had a snapshot of an agitated crowd; I wasn't about to start a riot.

> At one point or another we all are prodigals. I've been to the faraway lands of wasted living. I've slopped the hogs in the muck and mire of sin more than once—you have too.

The faces of those young men, squandering their inheritance in that faraway country of idolatry, are etched in my memory forever. I pray that eventually they will hear more of God's Word and will come to their senses. When that day comes all of Heaven will party!

Aha Moment #3

Back to Luke 15. The older brother had been working all day in the back forty, so when he returned home at the end of the workday he was surprised to find a party. In his confusion he asked one of the servants what was going on. Hearing that his good-for-nothing brother had returned and that Dad had thrown a party the likes of which he had never experienced, he was incredulous. He refused to even enter the house.

The kindly father left the party and pleaded with his elder son to join the celebration, but the normally mild-mannered, obedient, desperate-to-please firstborn exploded in anger: "Look! All these years I've been slaving for you and never disobeyed your orders. Yet you never gave me even a young goat so I could celebrate with my friends. But when this son of yours who has squandered your property with prostitutes comes home, you kill the fattened calf for him!" (vv. 29, 30).

Those listening to Jesus' surprising story must have thought, *Finally, someone shows up with common sense, a voice of reason in the insanity of unbridled waste and undisciplined forgiveness.* I suspect the crowd was relieved; now there would be a change in the outcome. *Surely this son will talk some sense into his father. Surely the father will realize the error of his ways. Surely the loser brother will be put in his proper place. Let justice be done!*

Then came the third aha moment in the story. Surprisingly, the direction of the narrative didn't change. The father, who loved his firstborn equally, remained a man of grace, not law. He reached out to his older son who in a sense was also lost—lost to the joy that comes through grace. Lost to his *own* need for grace. The father tenderly reminded his older son that everything in the estate was as good as his already. And then the father added emphatically, "But we had to celebrate and be glad, because this brother of yours was dead and is alive again; he was lost and is found" (v. 32). If Heaven in all its perfection can rejoice more over one sinner that comes home than all the faithful who stayed home, then so can we.

At one point or another we all are prodigals. I've been to the faraway lands of wasted living. I've slopped the hogs in the muck and mire of sin more than once—you have too. But despite our despicable past, God has graciously welcomed us home. We return to him in our tattered, foul rags, and he gives us his righteous white robe to cover our guilt. It is a wonderful moment of grace, not because we deserve it, but because grace is the Father's nature.

If the parable were simply a lesson about God's grace, it would still have no equal in literature. But it is more—it challenges us to reflect on the Father's heart as we reach out to others. Be gracious; there is no better way to surprise a justice-hungry world than with the forgiveness of God. But beware. As the years go by, and the memories of the faraway land where you have journeyed and squandered begin to fade, there is always the temptation to act like the older brother. May God forgive us when we do!

Thomas Wolfe was wrong. Because of God's grace, you *can* go home again!

1. "You can't go home again." What do you think about that statement? Have you ever attended a school reunion? What was it like to see former classmates again? Have you ever struggled with a restless spirit like the younger son did? How so?

2. Everyone's "faraway land" is different. List some practical steps you can take to resist the temptations that beckon you to your faraway land.

3. The younger son's desperate hunger for even pig's food triggered the change that brought him to his senses. What has it taken to bring you to your senses? Why is repentance so important in our relationship with God?

4. Define *grace*. Which seems easier to you—living in the freedom of grace or living by a list of dos and don'ts? Why? Why do so many people choose to live by the list? Does the fact that grace is *unfair* bother you? Why or why not?

Didn't See That Coming
For individual or group study

5. Charles Dickens said of this parable, "It is the finest short story ever written." Do you agree with his assessment? What makes it the finest: is it what happened in the heart of the younger son or what had been happening in the father's heart all along that makes the story so powerful? Explain your answer.

6. "Look! All these years I've been slaving for you and never disobeyed your orders. Yet you never gave me even a young goat so I could celebrate with my friends. But when this son of yours who has squandered your property with prostitutes comes home, you kill the fattened calf for him!" What do you think or feel when you hear these words of the older brother? Do you find yourself agreeing with him? empathizing with him? Why or why not? How can you avoid Older-Brother Syndrome?

Nothing is more noble, nothing more venerable than fidelity. Faithfulness and truth are the most sacred excellences and endowments of the human mind.

—CICERO

"Jesus entered Jericho and was passing through." So states the good doctor Luke (Luke 19:1). It was a short but significant visit.

Significant because his visit to Jericho that day was his last. Jesus passed through on his way to Jerusalem, where within days he would be crucified. Nearly fourteen centuries earlier, Joshua (Hebrew, meaning "savior") led the Israelites in the capture of Jericho. The fortified city walls fell with little human intervention; the people shouted, the trumpets blared, and God unleashed his power on the first city to succumb in the conquest of the promised land. As Jesus—the next Joshua—entered the city, he represented the hope of salvation and the anticipation of an eternal promised land.

It was a *significant* visit because, as he left Jericho that day, Jesus encountered Bartimaeus, a beggar who was blind. The old roadside beggar had spent his life relying on others' generous gifts, but when Jesus passed by,

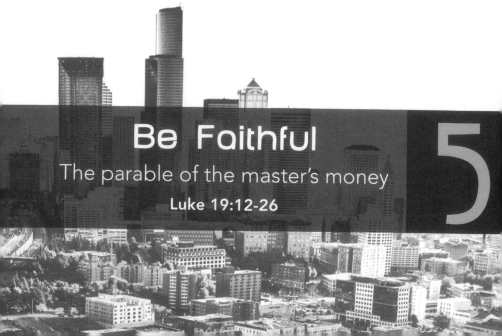

Be Faithful
The parable of the master's money
Luke 19:12-26

5

Bartimaeus seized the opportunity and pleaded with the healer for the gift of sight. When Jesus restored his vision, Bartimaeus's first glimpse was that of the face of God. He looked into those eyes of divine compassion and became an instant Christ follower.

A *significant* visit because in Jericho that day Jesus made a big deal over a little guy. The tax-collecting outcast, Zacchaeus, went out on a limb to meet the Savior and that encounter changed his life.

Significant—in Jericho that day Jesus told a surprising story that is often overlooked in the wake of the conversion of Zacchaeus. You might want to brush up on your math skills as this parable involves addition, multiplication, subtraction, and lots of numbers: one king, three responses, ten servants, fifteen cities, a hundred days' wages, and the challenge of unlimited faithfulness.

Believable Lies

Because Jesus was just passing through on his way to Jerusalem, the crowd that followed was giddy with excitement. The anticipation had been building for several months that the Messiah Jesus was finally going to overthrow the yoke of Roman oppression and restore the kingdom to Israel. Feeling the energy in the air, many were convinced the time of conquest had come. As is often the case, the people's expectations were not in sync with Jesus' explanation. While he certainly claimed to be the promised Messiah and God incarnate, he had never said anything to substantiate the age-old anticipation that the Messiah's kingdom would be an earthly reign. Even the disciples who spent three years of their lives with Jesus couldn't get past that expectancy.

We shouldn't be too critical though; it's amazing what people will believe. Though the evidence has provided us with the truth, some still believe the earth is flat, that the Apollo 11 moon landing was a government hoax, and that Elvis is still in the building. I heard about a lady who phoned the government to complain that the extra hour of sunlight from Daylight Saving Time was burning up her lawn! If you ask me, I'd say her clock was wound way too tight.

Be careful what you accept as true—the world is full of believable lies. Many dismissed Jesus in his day because he didn't measure up to the Messiah of their minds. Sadly, they missed the truth because they were fixated on a believable lie. To set the record straight, Jesus told this parable about a master's money.

Of Kings, Riches, and Investments

"A man of noble birth went to a distant country to have himself appointed king and then to return. . . . But his subjects hated him and sent a delegation after him to say, 'We don't want this man to be our king'" (Luke 19:12, 14).

> This parable involves addition, multiplication, subtraction, and lots of numbers.

Jesus barely introduced the story, and the people were already smiling or snickering. This very scenario had actually happened, and Jesus' listeners knew it. When Herod the Great (king at the time of Jesus' birth) died, there was a dispute over his will as to which of his sons would rule in his place. Both Archelaus and Antipas hurried to Rome to present their cases before Caesar. Caesar compromised by giving both sons areas of rule, but did not at that time grant the title of king to either. A few years later (AD 6) a delegation of Jews approached Caesar to protest the harsh and brutal treatment suffered by the Judean people under the leadership of Archelaus. As a result, Caesar deposed and banished Archelaus to Vienne, never again to be a source of pain to the Jews.[1] A quarter of a century later, as Jesus began his story, the image of the ousted king would have brought a smile to their faces.

Jesus' story line took an abrupt departure from this historical event, however, as the parable's nobleman returned home having been crowned king *despite* the people's objections. Regardless of the similarities, Jesus wasn't telling the tale of a Roman king—he was telling his own. Rejected by the very people he came to save, he will nonetheless return as King of kings. This parable's theme of faithfulness is set against an eschatological backdrop. Since that day when Jesus first told this surprising story, each reader must evaluate his own faithfulness in light of the King's return. If he comes before you finish reading this chapter, will he find you faithful?

As the nobleman prepared to go away, he divided up some of his wealth among his servants so that his work would not suffer in his absence. "So he called ten of his servants and gave them ten minas. 'Put this money to work,' he said, 'until I come back'" (v. 13).

All ten servants were given equal amounts of money. A mina was equivalent to a hundred days' wages. Let's put that in terms we can understand. Based on the current work week of five days and an annual salary of $40,000, a hundred days' wages would be equivalent to $16,000. From my perspective that's a sizable sum.

> When God sees you being faithful with little, he will know you can be trusted with much.

Suppose your boss gave you a check for $16,000 with the instructions to "put this money to work." He takes off on some entrepreneurial adventure, but you know he will return with the expectation of collecting more money than he gave you. The pressure is on. How will you invest, save, or spend that $16,000 to make the boss proud? That was the dilemma the servants in the parable faced. It's our dilemma as well.

Be Faithful with What You Have

None of the ten would have argued with the master regarding the amount, but I suspect there was a mixed reaction among the servants concerning this endowment. Some may have considered it too little to work with—they had big ideas, and a single mina wouldn't have been enough capital to get their dream off the ground. Others, however, may have experienced panic attacks at being responsible for so much of someone else's money. What if their investment venture failed? What if they lost every last mite? How could they possibly repay the master? The gift may have been the same for all ten servants, but the reaction certainly wasn't.

Matthew recorded a similar parable that Jesus told in Jerusalem during the week leading up to his crucifixion. It differed in that varying amounts were distributed to the servants. One received five talents, another two talents, and yet a third only one talent. Such a distribution could create an even greater consternation among the servants. It's easy to imagine both the one- and two-talent servants being jealous of the five-talent recipient. Jealousy can consume one's joy, contentment, and positive spirit. And when cultivated through contemplation or fertilized by others' encouragement, jealousy can grow into resentment, bitterness, and anger.

It's also easy to imagine the five-talent servant being ensnared by pride: *The master gave me more than any of the other servants—I must be special.* Yet in this tale, having more does not indicate a greater privilege bestowed by the master, but a greater responsibility owed to the master.

I suppose it would be nice if everyone were gifted equally, but that is an unrealistic expectation. Face it; life isn't fair. There are probably some with higher intellects, greater abilities, and better personalities than you. Conversely, there are those who look at you with a twinge of envy. We are all gifted differently, and we should strive to gratefully accept what we've received from God, and be faithful with it. God doesn't have to give you a hundred days' wages or five talents for you to be able to make a difference. Be faithful with what you have—the little things—and when God sees you being faithful with little, he will know you can be trusted with much.

Be Faithful to God's Instructions

The nobleman's instructions to his servants were simple—and the same for all ten. "Put this to work while I am gone; I'll expect results when I return." It was his money after all, and he had every right to expect a return on his investment. There could hardly be any confusion about the mission in general—the challenge came in devising a specific plan of action.

Generally, God's instructions to us start out simple, clear, and understandable. Whatever the reason, we tend to complicate them as we implement them. Consider for a moment the Great Commission to the church, "Go and make disciples of all nations" (Matthew 28:19). That's pretty straightforward. Jesus even included some strategic helps: teach, baptize, and then teach some more. Again, nothing too complicated about that. So why after 2,000 years are we still struggling to accomplish the mission?

There are a lot of contributing factors—sketchy methodology, weary indifference, divisions over nonessentials, self-centered desires that have eclipsed true vision, traditions that have become monuments to the past instead of momentum for the future, and more. Mostly we've just stopped being faithful to God's instructions. When God tells us who, what, where, and why, that should be a sufficient call to action.

Instructions matter. Like most men I'm fairly confident that I can put whatever together without the instruction manual. I wish I had back all the time I've wasted in disassembling things that had too many leftover parts because I didn't start with the instructions. I'm learning though. Last Christmas my wife, Elsie, and I bought our first GPS to use when we travel. It has already saved us considerable time and anxiety, but on a recent outing to a familiar area, I was convinced the GPS was wrong. (It's a sad day when a grown man argues with the electronic voice of the GPS.) Nevertheless, I reluctantly followed its lead with the intention of being able to celebrate an I-told-you-so moment later. As I'm sure you've already guessed, *I* was wrong. I learned a much more efficient way to get us to our destination, simply by following the instructions.

Sometimes reading the instructions spells the difference between life and death. Every pilot knows to monitor the panel—instruments don't lie. The instructional information gleaned from the altimeter, airspeed indicator, artificial horizon, rate of climb, fuel gauges, and compass can make the difference between a final approach to a safe landing and truly your final approach.

God desires us to do as he says, not just because he is our Master, but because he loves us and wants what is best for us. Most of our Father's instructions don't need explanation, just application. You may remember the story of the Aramean military commander, Naaman, who searched out the prophet Elisha to be cleansed of his leprosy (2 Kings 5). He was somewhat dismayed at traveling to Samaria in his quest for healing, but when Elisha didn't even bother to go to the door when he arrived, he was steamed.

Elisha merely sent a messenger with the instructions to dip seven times in the Jordan River. These were not complicated instructions. They were very simple. Yet a ticked-off Naaman was ready to head home. There had to be more to it than a dip in the river! After all, there were better rivers in Aram; he despised the muddy Jordan.

As Naaman prepared for retreat, his wise servants approached him with logic he could not refute: "My father, if the prophet had told you to do some great thing, would you not have done it? How much more, then, when he tells you, 'Wash and be cleansed'!" (5:13). With little to lose, he reluctantly headed for the Jordan with the intention of being able to celebrate an I-told-you-so moment after his bath. Up and down six times; Naaman had to be thinking it was a hoax. Then came the seventh dip. When he broke the surface of the water, his skin had been restored to that of a young boy. Since leprosy would normally have been a death sentence, Naaman's response to his healing was exuberant: "Now I know that there is no God in all the world except in Israel" (v. 15). Imagine the tragic ending if he had angrily sloshed out of the Jordan after only six dips. God's instructions matter!

> Most of our Father's instructions don't need explanation, just application.

Back to our narrative in Luke 19. When the nobleman—now turned king—returned, he called for his servants to give an account of their responsibility (vv. 16-19):

> The first one came and said, "Sir, your mina has earned ten more."
> "Well done, my good servant!" his master replied. "Because you have been trustworthy in a very small matter, take charge of ten cities."
> The second came and said, "Sir, your mina has earned five more."
> His master answered, "You take charge of five cities."

The king did not seem more thrilled with the ten minas earned by the first servant over the five earned by the second. Both received identical praise and compensatory rewards. The king was not seeking success as much as loyal obedience. The exaggerated reward seemed out of proportion with what each servant had accomplished. It's one thing to earn ten minas but something quite spectacular to be given authority over ten cities. Is it possible that Jesus overstated the contrast? I hardly think so. I anticipate that Heaven will be a greatly exaggerated reward in comparison to our meager kingdom accomplishments in this life. If anything, Jesus' analogy is understated.

Until the King returns, he has provided us with simple instructions for daily living in his kingdom; they are an efficient way to get us to our destination—a life of faithfulness. Consider just a few of his remarkable precepts:

- Love one another as I have loved you.
- Go the second mile, turn the other cheek, and love your enemies.
- Do for others as you would have them do for you.
- Pray without ceasing.
- Encourage one another all the more as you see the day approaching.
- Remember your body is the temple of the Holy Spirit.
- Avoid the very appearance of evil.
- Give thanks in all circumstances.
- Rejoice in the Lord always.
- Love the Lord your God with all your heart, soul, mind, and strength.

God's instructions matter. Follow them faithfully.

Be Faithful with All Your Heart

The first servants to be interrogated had honored the king's wishes and wisely invested his money to earn a profit. Nothing surprising about that—it was predictable. Just when Jesus' audience thought they had the story figured out, Jesus inverted the outcome with the introduction of the less-than-noble third servant. The crowd didn't see *that* coming. Listen to the exchange (vv. 20-23):

Then another servant came and said, "Sir, here is your mina; I have kept it laid away in a piece of cloth. I was afraid of you, because you are a hard man. You take out what you did not put in and reap what you did not sow."

His master replied, "I will judge you by your own words, you wicked servant! You knew, did you, that I am a hard man, taking out what I did not put in, and reaping what I did not sow? Why then didn't you put my money on deposit, so that when I came back, I could have collected it with interest?"

This guy was foolish, lazy, and perhaps spiteful. First of all, Tweedle Dumb explained that he had hidden the mina in a rag—a worthless piece of scrap cloth. In that day, wrapping cash in a perishable piece of cloth was considered one of the most irresponsible ways to take care of money.[2] To treat the king's capital with such disregard was indeed foolish; for the man to admit that's what he had done was just plain stupid. To preserve and protect the money he should have locked it in a strongbox or stored it in the temple treasury, much like we would use a lockbox at the local bank.

> Until the King returns, he has provided us with simple instructions for daily living in his kingdom.

If stupidity wasn't his claim to fame, perhaps it was laziness. Let's assume he wasn't too creative (that shouldn't require much imagination) and he simply could not think of a good investment plan. At the very least he should have deposited the money at a bank so it would have earned interest during the king's absence. When called to account, the lazy servant claimed fear of his boss as his excuse for failure.

There is another theory—the one I like best—that depicts this servant as treacherously spiteful. He didn't like the nobleman to begin with and really didn't expect him to be elevated to king. In his mind the odds of the nobleman's return were slim to nil, so after a sufficient wait, the mina would be his. But the newly crowned king *did* return, and the servant's plan was foiled. In his frustration he derided the king's ethics by accusing him of misappropriating funds.[3]

Jesus concluded the parable (vv. 24-27):

> Then he said to those standing by, "Take his mina away from him and give it to the one who has ten minas."
> "Sir," they said, "he already has ten!"
> He replied, "I tell you that to everyone who has, more will be given, but as for the one who has nothing, even what he has will be taken away. But those enemies of mine who did not want me to be king over them—bring them here and kill them in front of me."

> **God has been and continues to be faithful to us. How can we be anything less in return?**

What's the primary lesson of Jesus' narrative? As the parable unfolds, one gets the distinct impression that the lesson is about wise investing that leads to a profit. However, the tragic response of the third servant changes the whole course of the story. Here is the profound truth Jesus was teaching: unfaithfulness is failure. The faithless servant's mina was taken away and given to the one who had demonstrated great faithfulness.

Don't miss this truth. God does not expect us all to rise to a particular level of intellect—there is no minimum score on your spiritual SAT test before you can apply to serve God. And God does not expect us all to achieve a specific number of accomplishments—there is no minimum quota of encouraging words spoken, cups of cold water given, or second miles traveled before God will use us.

God *does* expect us all to be faithful—no exceptions. Faithfulness transcends talent, personality, intellect, looks, opportunity, advantages, obstacles, and any other conceivable excuse we might offer God for our failure to carry out his mission.

Unfaithfulness Is a Disease

We must guard against the highly contagious TSS (Third-Servant Syndrome). Left unchecked it can be deadly, but the symptoms are easily recognized.

Nauseating complacency

Complacency is "a feeling of quiet pleasure or security, often while unaware of some potential danger, defect, or the like; self-satisfaction or smug satisfaction with an existing situation, condition, etc."[4] The servant didn't really expect the king to return, so he became lackadaisical in fulfilling his responsibilities. Can you relate?

Complacent Christians think things like: *Two thousand years have come and gone since Jesus told this parable, and he hasn't returned yet. What's the hurry? I've got plenty of time to invest my life into something significant.* Jesus had a word for such tepid loyalty—"lukewarm." And such lukewarm Christianity made him sick (Revelation 3:16)!

Fractured excuses

Alexander Pope is thought to have said, "An excuse is worse than a lie, for an excuse is a lie, guarded." When caught in our sin, we immediately become defensive and begin offering up some lame excuses: "If only I hadn't been so busy," "If only I had someone to help me," "If only I had the kind of talent like so-and-so," "If only I was more mature," "If only I was younger," "If only the dog hadn't eaten my only copy of the Bible." Like a badly fractured femur, lame excuses leave us nothing to stand on.

Feverish spite

At times life doesn't unfold like we planned it, and we have no one to blame but God. Perhaps God answered your prayers with a no instead of a yes. Maybe you've been a believer for years, but now you are battling cancer and the disease is winning. Whatever your disappointment, it may cause you to feel a bit spiteful toward God. *If God is going to treat me this way after all I've done for him, well . . . I just won't serve him!* Don't let that happen to you. We live in a broken world, but not one broken by God's hand. Despite the fact that our sin ruined his perfect creation, God has been and continues to be faithful to us. How can we be anything less in return?

The vaccination

Faithfulness is the only lasting vaccination for TSS. Consider one example.

The young Indian preacher stood only as tall as my shoulder, but he cast a long shadow of faithfulness. Emmanuel and I shared a common faith and desire to preach the gospel, but that's where our similarities ended. I cannot describe in words the impact he made on my life and ministry, but I can tell you his story.

> I pray that our faithfulness will also warrant such heavenly praise.

Christian preachers in India are often the subject of persecution due to the overwhelming influence of Hinduism. I've learned, however, that the threat of persecution does not diminish the power of their proclamation. Emmanuel and his wife moved to an unreached area specifically for the purpose of spreading the gospel of Christ. Early on in their ministry, Hindu extremists attacked their small, fledgling congregation during a Sunday worship service. The terrified people fled in all directions. The thugs then took Emmanuel and his pregnant wife and beat them terribly. They produced what appeared to be legal papers, demanding that they renounce their faith. Both refused.

That's when the nightmare went from bad to worse.

They tied Emmanuel to a tree and forced him to watch as the extremists took turns raping his wife, all the while demanding that he recant his faith. Throughout the horrendous ordeal, Emmanuel's wife pleaded with him not to give in to their demands and not to give up on Christ. Before all her attackers could complete the dastardly deed, her screams drew the attention of others in the surrounding area. Village folks came to their aid, and the persecutors fled so they would not be recognized. By that time Emmanuel had lost consciousness, and both he and his wife were rushed to the hospital.

The physical wounds healed normally; the mental and emotional wounds healed much more slowly. Had that been me, I would have packed my bags and moved my family as far away from those awful memories as possible. I suspect as my wounds healed, I would have nursed a bitter grudge against such cruel and heartless men and plotted my revenge. At the very least I would have taken a chapter out of David's imprecatory psalms and prayed hard against my enemies.

Not Emmanuel. He and his wife remained in the same area, continued to work with the same people, and faithfully preached the same gospel of grace. I wish I could have met Emmanuel's wife; he credits her faith as the strong one. God honors such faithfulness. In the years that followed, the church where Emmanuel ministered grew to a congregation of seven hundred, and he and others who ministered with him planted seven new churches.

Then came that fateful Sunday when five of the rapists showed up in front of the congregation again. That Sunday, however, they had come to be baptized into Christ Jesus.

I heard Emmanuel tell this story. Never before or since have I been so overwhelmed and humbled by one couple's faithfulness to God. Emmanuel has since gone home to be with the Lord, the result of a tragic auto accident. Like the saints of old, his faithfulness stands far taller than his diminutive stature. The memory of his enduring loyalty to Jesus Christ still challenges me to grow stronger in my personal commitment. Emmanuel took his mina and earned *at least* ten more. I'm confident he heard those immortal words as he stepped across the threshold of eternity, "Well done, my good servant!" When the time comes, I pray that our faithfulness will also warrant such heavenly praise.

1. "God doesn't have to give you a hundred days' wages or five talents for you to be able to make a difference. Be faithful with what you have." How would you assess your giftedness for kingdom work? Are you satisfied with your gifts and talents or would you prefer some that others have? In what ways are you currently using your gifts to further God's work on this earth?

2. What are some other ways in which you could faithfully use your gifts for God? What are some things you've always dreamed of doing for others, but haven't tried?

3. "Most of our Father's instructions don't need explanation, just application." Do you agree? Are God's instructions clear or do they need revision? How can we be faithful in the way we interpret God's commands?

Didn't See That Coming
For individual or group study

4. Name some of God's instructions you find challenging to follow. What factors make following God's instructions difficult
   for you?

5. "The tragic response of the third servant changes the whole
   course of the story. Here is the profound truth Jesus was teaching: unfaithfulness is failure." Have you ever been lazy in your
   service to God? How have you failed to use what he gave you?
   How can you be truly faithful to God with all your heart?

Our son-in-law Errek is an excellent golfer, and for Christmas he put a Titleist putter on his wish list. That particular putter was a hot seller during the holidays, so to make sure we bought just the right one, I asked our daughter Rebekah for help. She found a great bargain on the Internet, and the deal was made. It was beautiful (as putters go)—looked identical to the pictures in the ads. We were ready for Christmas.

Then early in December, Rebekah received an e-mail from the seller asking us to return the club because it was a phony. Being the trusting individual that I am, I was convinced we were being conned. After all, these clubs were in high demand. I figured it this way: the seller anticipated we would return the "fake" putter that he in turn would resell. He'd make double the profit, and we would never see a refund. Besides, I was still not convinced it was a fraud; I had studied the serial numbers and pictures on the Titleist website and was persuaded we had the real thing. Just to make sure, however, I called Titleist and explained

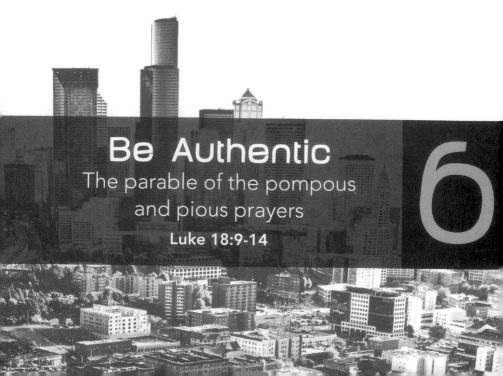

Be Authentic
The parable of the pompous and pious prayers
Luke 18:9-14

6

the problem. Was there any way to test the putter to see if we had the real McCoy? The customer service agent told me to give it the magnet test. An authentic Titleist putter is made of stainless steel, and since magnets won't adhere to stainless, we'd know soon enough.

I grabbed a magnet and *thunk,* it stuck to that putter head like cockle-burs on a long-haired dog. My heart sank—we'd been duped. I considered giving Errek the cheaper, fake putter anyway and telling him to keep it away from magnets, but I couldn't bring myself to give him a phony. And yes, we did find an authentic one (at a higher price) just in time for Christmas. It passed the magnet test too! We all learned a valuable lesson that Christmas—authenticity matters!

Challenging the Self-Righteous

What's true of putters is even truer of people. No one likes being around phony, self-righteous hypocrites. Jesus had to contend with such behavior frequently in his earthly ministry, and the occasion for this parable is one such example. Dr. Luke introduced this parable with the following preface: "To some who were confident of their own righteousness and looked down on everybody else, Jesus told this parable" (Luke 18:9). We aren't given specifics about his listeners, but they probably should have joined AA—Arrogance Anonymous.

Scripture does not always provide us with such a clear context for the telling of a parable. It is never easy to confront the sin of pride, but in this case, Jesus—the master of confrontation—used a simple but surprising parable to challenge his self-righteous audience. (vv. 10-14):

> Two men went up to the temple to pray, one a Pharisee and the other a tax collector. The Pharisee stood up and prayed about himself: "God, I thank you that I am not like other men—robbers, evildoers, adulterers—or even like this tax collector. I fast twice a week and give a tenth of all I get."
> But the tax collector stood at a distance. He would not even look up to heaven, but beat his breast and said, "God, have mercy on me, a sinner."

I tell you that this man, rather than the other, went home justified before God. For everyone who exalts himself will be humbled, and he who humbles himself will be exalted.

The crowd would not have been surprised at two men praying in the temple; that happened every day. But by the end of the story, Jesus' listeners were in a state of shock. To understand why, we need to study the characters in this parable. Jesus picked polar opposites to play out this drama.

The Pharisee

Since the time of Christ, the word *Pharisee* has had a rather negative connotation. Our English adjective *pharisaical* grows out of the haughty and hypocritical attitude of this group. To be called pharisaical is painfully insulting; no one wants to be accused of acting like the Pharisees.

The Pharisees, however, didn't start out this way. For the most part, they were members of the middle class. Most tended to be businessmen—the merchants and tradesmen of the times. Most would not have been formally educated in the Law, though they loved God's law. Regarding the general populace, Pharisees championed the cause of human equality; in many respects they represented a democratic movement. Their original intent seems admirable: to bring every area of life into subjection to the law of God.[1]

> We all learned a valuable lesson that Christmas—authenticity matters!

By the time of Christ, the Pharisees' sect had evolved into more of an elite group with an aloof attitude. But not all had become corrupted. Nicodemus and Joseph of Arimathea, who tenderly interred the crucified body of Jesus in Joseph's new tomb, were likely both Pharisees. And consider for a moment—any Pharisee who had remained true to the original intent would have made a great neighbor: middle class, hard worker, champion of human equality, lover of democratic principles, genuinely devoted to keeping God's law to the best of his ability. That's the kind of guy a dad wants his daughter to marry!

Sometimes we start off with the best of intentions, but somewhere along the way our pride derails us. We get sidetracked, lose focus, and suddenly all sense of authenticity disappears. So often in history well-intentioned revolutionaries have battled the tyranny of a despotic regime only to become a tyrannical regime themselves. The noble cause is lost, and authenticity is sacrificed on the altar of self-centered power and control. It is easy to be critical of the Pharisees—but at times we are no better.

> When Jesus told this parable, his audience would have expected the Pharisee to be the hero and the tax collector to be the villain.

The Tax Collector

Some translations refer to the second man as a publican, which means a "collector of public revenues." Doesn't matter what you call him, he's still a tax collector. Is there any period of human history when *tax collector* had a positive ring to it?

While touring Washington, D.C., by bus, we passed the headquarters of the dreaded IRS—the Internal Revenue Service. The tour guide pointed at the building constructed with Indiana limestone and commented that it was the most hated building in D.C. Usually, I'm thrilled to learn that a building of national importance used Indiana limestone. Not this time. I felt a collective shudder pass through the bus as we drove by. Did you hear about the man who on his deathbed called his best friend and asked him to be responsible for his ashes following his cremation? "What do you want me to do with them," the friend asked. "Package them up, mail them to the IRS and write on the envelope, 'Now you have everything!'"[2]

Honestly, I have known some really good people who worked for the IRS, but they lived under a shadow they could never shake.

If you think our attitude toward tax collectors is bad, it comes in a distant second to the hatred Jewish people felt for those Hebrews who collected revenues for the Roman government. With little accountability and every opportunity to line their pockets with extorted funds, tax collectors were understandably despised. None of the tax money stayed in Judea; all went to support the Roman Empire.[3] Not only were most tax collectors known as fraudulently deceptive, they also were spiritually defiled because of their continual contact with Gentiles. A tax collector could not testify in a Jewish court of law, nor could he tithe to the temple treasury in Jerusalem. A good Jewish man would never ask a tax collector for change, because he believed the publican's money was unclean. So when Jesus told this parable, his audience would have expected the Pharisee to be the hero and the tax collector to be the villain.

Prayer is the setting for the parable, but authenticity is its theme. The heart of the story is not about talking to God, but about being authentic in the presence of God and others. According to Merriam-Webster.com, *authenticity* is being "true to one's own personality, spirit, or character"; not false, fake, or phony, but real. The biblical virtue of authenticity has long been an expectation in the lives of those who follow God. For instance, God spoke to his people through the prophet Amos about their worship: "I hate all your show and pretense—the hypocrisy of your religious festivals and solemn assemblies" (Amos 5:21, *NLT*).

Paul wrote to his son in the faith, Timothy, on the purpose of teaching: "The purpose of my instruction is that all believers would be filled with love that comes from a pure heart, a clear conscience, and genuine faith" (1 Timothy 1:5, *NLT*).

Peter wrote to encourage the church living on the ragged edge of persecution: "In this you greatly rejoice, though now for a little while you may have had to suffer grief in all kinds of trials. These have come so that your faith—of greater worth than gold, which perishes even though refined by fire—may be proved genuine and may result in praise, glory and honor when Jesus Christ is revealed" (1 Peter 1:6, 7). "So get rid of all evil behavior. Be done with all deceit, hypocrisy, jealousy, and all unkind speech" (1 Peter 2:1, *NLT*).

In worship, in discipleship, and in the tough times of life, there is the expectation that everything we do as Christians will be authentic, genuine, and without pretense. Simply put, be real—nobody likes a fake. We long for authentic friends, authentic relationships, authentic leadership, and authentic love. So how does a twenty-first-century disciple of Jesus grow and develop a spirit of authenticity? There may be many ways, but Jesus highlights three essentials in this parable.

Humility

Two men went up to the temple to pray. One looked around and prayed about himself. One looked down and prayed for himself.

There are several right ways to pray. I prefer to close my eyes (except, of course, when I pray in the car). I need all the help I can get in shutting out the distractions. If I could, I would close my ears too. Others lift their open eyes upward and pray while focused on Heaven. Some sit, some kneel, some stand—all are acceptable. There is, however, one method that will be sure to lose your focus—praying while looking around to see who is watching and listening. Positive answers seem hard to come by when we pray that way.

Jesus said this in the Sermon on the Mount: "And when you pray, do not be like the hypocrites, for they love to pray standing in the synagogues and on the street corners to be seen by men. I tell you the truth, they have received their reward in full. But when you pray, go into your room, close the door and pray to your Father, who is unseen. Then your Father, who sees what is done in secret, will reward you" (Matthew 6:5, 6).

The Pharisee in the story made quite a show of his prayer time. He stood and looked around—no other way to see the tax collector over in the corner—and began to pontificate loudly enough for all to hear. The *NIV* states that he prayed "about himself," but it would be more accurate to say he prayed *to* himself. He sought nothing from God in his prayer other than a pat on the back. While *God* appeared only once in the Pharisee's prayer, the pronoun *I* popped up multiple times.

The Pharisee may have received some adoring glances from worshippers within earshot of his prayer, but it's hard to believe his hot-air prayer traveled any higher than the temple ceiling.

Enter the tax collector. He didn't look around to see who was in attendance. He didn't look up in a show of piety. He simply looked down in humiliation and beat on his sinful chest. He asked for something that only God could provide; thus God was honored by such faith. He didn't pray for more money, greater respect, or a faster chariot. He prayed for God's mercy! I suspect his prayer was whispered, but it echoed through the corridors of Heaven. God heard every word clearly.

Humility matters. How about the guy who was voted the most humble pastor in America? To mark the occasion, his congregation gave him a gold medal engraved with: "To the most humble pastor in America." The next Sunday he wore it proudly, and they took it back![4]

These words from Romans are worth remembering daily: "Do not think of yourself more highly than you ought" (Romans 12:3). We could also say, "Don't make yourself out to be more lowly than you are to get attention." Either attitude is bound to repel people. Authentic humility, however, is one of the most attractive virtues. Whether you are addressing God or other people, remember that humility goes a long way.

> There is, however, one method that will be sure to lose your focus—praying while looking around to see who is watching and listening.

Recently, legendary UCLA basketball coach John Wooden died at age ninety-nine. If any coach could have justifiably been proud, it was John Wooden; but it was his gentle, humble nature that endeared him to scores of players and thousands of fans. One of his favorite maxims was this: "There is nothing stronger than gentleness."[5] The humble, gentle Christian demonstrates an enduring, impressive strength.

Honesty

Two men went up to the temple to pray. One looked outward and assumed the worst in others. One looked inward and saw the worst in himself.

Not only did this Pharisee lack a humble spirit, he also lacked the ability to take an honest look at himself. He wasn't as good as he suggested. No man is. To hear him pray, you would have thought him perfect. Are we to conclude that he never had a lustful thought, lashed out with an angry tone, or ate a gluttonous meal? Had this Pharisee never misjudged another's heart? From his prayer we know he did exactly that. It appears that he may have scanned the audience before offering his prayerful critique (maybe he made a broad sweeping gesture with his hands): "God, I thank you that I am not like other men—robbers, evildoers, adulterers . . ." Had he spotted men in the temple that he believed to be guilty of such behavior? *There stands Reuben on the other side of the room. He borrowed a loaf of bread from my wife last year and never paid that back. Robber! Look at Isaac putting his offering in the treasury—why, there's not enough guilt money in all Judea to compensate for his nasty streak. And who could miss ol' Zachariah kissin' up to the priest—I hear he's been doing a lot of kissin' up lately.*

> The Pharisee's entire praise offering was filled with wrong assumptions.

As I read this parable, I can just see Mr. Pious point behind him (as if God didn't know who was standing in the corner praying) and express feigned thanks that he wasn't like that disgusting tax collector. He made the assumption that, because his fellow pray-er was a tax collector, he was beyond the scope of grace. Maybe he intended to apply all three derogatory terms to the publican: he was a robber to be sure, evil in his actions, and an adulterer (spiritually, if not physically). The Pharisee's entire praise offering was filled with wrong assumptions. He could not have known the publican's heart, and he seemed to be blissfully unaware of the state of his own.

Assumption is a dangerous thing. When you incorrectly assume something to be true, you will always be surprised at the inverted outcome.

Some years ago I was returning home late one afternoon from an out-of-town meeting. Traffic on the four-lane road was moving at a reasonable pace except for the aging, faded red pickup in the right-hand lane. As I neared the old truck, I noticed the driver through the dust-streaked back glass. He appeared somewhat stoop-shouldered as he manhandled the steering wheel with his left arm. His dull flannel shirt had seen better days, and his sweat-stained farmer's cap had tufts of gray hair sticking out all around the bottom of the brim. His right arm was not resting on the steering wheel but was draped around the shoulders of a curly-haired blonde. From my vantage point—which was closing rapidly—she appeared far too young to be sitting that close. Was this one of those May/December relationships that just doesn't make sense? What does a young blonde see in an old geezer anyway?

As I pulled around to pass, I couldn't help but glance over into the cab of the truck. Imagine my shock when it was not a young blonde that returned my glance, but a golden-haired retriever sitting next to his master. I swear the dog winked at me as if to say, "Surprise!" What had moments before appeared to be a twisted courtship was simply an endearing picture of friendship between an old farmer and his best four-legged friend. I learned a valuable lesson that day about assumptions—don't make them!

The tax collector's prayer was not long or flowery, but like a double-edged sword, it cut to the heart of the issue. He assumed nothing; he knew who and what he was—a sinner. All of us are sinners, but honestly recognizing that fact takes a person genuinely devoted to God. Ironic, isn't it? The Pharisee, who would have been considered one of the most honest members of society, was neither honest with himself nor with God. The tax collector, who was viewed with revulsion for his dishonesty, was both honest with himself and with God. Without honesty, authenticity is impossible.

Holiness

Two men went up to the temple to pray. One was confident he couldn't be more righteous. One was confident he needed to be more righteous.

The word *Pharisee* actually comes from a word that means "to be separate."

The Pharisees prided themselves on being separate from the average man on the street when it came to knowing, cherishing, and obeying God's Word; thus they viewed themselves as more righteous.

The Pharisee in this parable was convinced that his holiness was as good as it gets, and he wanted everyone to know it. Though the law required only an annual fast (Leviticus 23:26-29; Numbers 29:7), he boasted of fasting twice a week. The Pharisees generally fasted on Mondays and Thursdays. This was not required of them, but the public market opened on these days so more people would have been in town.[6] If you want to brag, it helps to have a crowd! He verbally paraded his days of fasting and his obedience in giving. As a rule the Pharisees were notorious for tithing everything, giving attention even to the smallest of spice seeds (Matthew 23:23). Mr. Pious wanted folks to know his good deeds. Jesus had something to say about these: "Be careful not to do your 'acts of righteousness' before men, to be seen by them. If you do, you will have no reward from your Father in heaven" (Matthew 6:1).

The Pharisee's holier-than-thou attitude is best expressed by Rabbi Simeon ben Jochai, "If there are only two righteous men in the world, I and my son are these two; if there is only one, I am he!"[7] If Jesus resisted the self-righteousness of the Pharisees, what would he say to us today?

In contrast to the Pharisee, the tax collector moved away from the crowd and stood alone at a distance. He genuinely separated himself from the crowd so he could focus on God. His prayer was not for public ears; he had nothing to parade before the public's eye. He was in desperate need of God's merciful forgiveness so he could become a man of righteousness.

What a contrast between these two pray-ers! One boasted of his perfection; one confessed his imperfection. Only one prayed for a holy result—to be separated from the guilt of his sin.

I see one more twist of irony in this parable—the words *holy, holiness,* and *saint* all come from the same root word that means "separate." It means to be separate for good. The Pharisee, who exalted himself as being separate from everyone and everything common, missed out on the true separation—holiness. The tax collector, who separated himself from the crowd in the temple, demonstrated more spiritual holiness—by being authentic.

When the word *holy* is used to describe someone today, the image that typically jumps to mind is a dour, prune-faced, old-fashioned, boring Christian. Wrong picture. Holiness is a state of being set apart—being separated for the purpose of doing or being good, for devotion to God. Being holy doesn't mean acting holier-than-thou; it means recognizing the one who is holier-than-you (and everyone) and devoting yourself to follow his example.

Authentic holiness reaches out to help others while expecting nothing in return.

Authentic holiness gives generously because there is a pressing need.

Authentic holiness loves unconditionally.

Authentic holiness encourages.

> If Jesus resisted the self-righteousness of the Pharisees, what would he say to us today?

You can ask God to help you to be holy—to separate yourself not from people, but from every attitude that is mediocre, negative, and coarse. Be different, not by attracting attention to yourself, but by who and what you give your attention. Encourage others in their walk of faith by being honest about your own. Reach out with no expectations; love with no strings attached. Be authentic. Without authenticity, holiness is impossible.

The Bottom Line

Two men went up to the temple to pray. One went home just the same. One went home justified.

The exalted one was humbled; the humble one was exalted. Authenticity matters!

Errek tells me the authentic Titleist putter works like a charm. I've watched him drop some pretty impressive putts while using it. I'm not surprised. When you put an authentic putter in the hands of a great golfer, good things happen. You might say that's just par for the course.

What's true of putters is even truer of people. When you put an authentic Christian in the hands of our great God, good things happen!

1. "Authenticity matters!" Has there ever been an occasion when you were duped? How did it make you feel and what was your response? Are you more guarded as a result? How so?

2. I'm sure most of us can think of someone we know who is like the Pharisee in this parable. What is your attitude toward such a person? What character traits make him or her difficult to be around?

3. "Do not think of yourself more highly than you ought" (Romans 12:3). How would you describe humility? How do you know if you are humble enough? List the qualities you think make for a humble character, or list examples of actions that reflect humility.

Didn't See That Coming
For individual or group study

4. "The tax collector's prayer was not long or flowery, but like a double-edged sword, it cut to the heart of the issue. He assumed nothing; he knew who and what he was—a sinner." Why do we have such a hard time being honest with ourselves? Is it possible to be genuine and self-deceived at the same time? Explain your answer.

5. How have you been guilty of making assumptions about others? Why are assumptions so dangerous?

6. What image comes to your mind when you hear the word holiness? How are holiness and authenticity connected?

Street-smart—having the shrewd resourcefulness needed to survive in an urban environment.
—THE FREE DICTIONARY

There are at least two kinds of smarts: book smarts and street smarts. People who tend to rely on what they learned in a classroom, lecture hall, or quiet library are said to have book smarts. At times book-smart people may seem out of touch with the general flow of humanity or lacking in common sense. Street-smart people, on the other hand, are those who survive in a slightly more hostile environment, where practicality is a necessity. Sometimes street-smart people come across as gruff, guarded, and skeptical; they rely more on lessons learned via personal experiences rather than for pop quizzes. In their extreme forms, the two are like oil and water—they don't mix well.

A nice blend of the two smarts is preferable, but we are seldom so equally balanced. However, both pale in comparison to being Book-smart—that's *book* with a capital *B*. Miss out on God's Word and it won't matter how smart you are. Perhaps that's why Jesus' audience found the story we'll study in this chapter so challenging; the main character of this parable (found

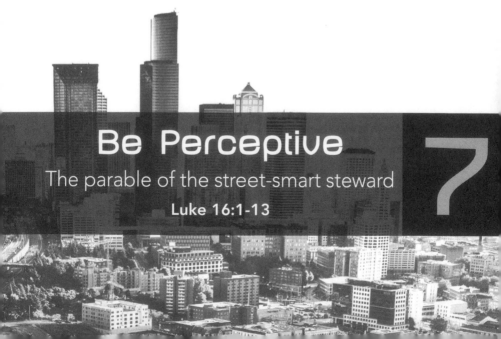

Be Perceptive
The parable of the street-smart steward
Luke 16:1-13

7

only in the Gospel of Luke) relied on his street smarts. His actions grew out of his experience, not God's expertise. His plan was designed to protect his immediate prospects, not his ultimate future. One would expect the hero of Jesus' parable to be a truth seeker, not a slick deceiver.

A Plan of Action

Like Einstein's theory of relativity, this parable can be hard to understand. If you've mastered $E=mc^2$ or the concept of quantum physics, good for you. I'm still puzzling over much smaller issues.

> Do we really understand the story?
> Do we really understand the Savior?

But this story from Luke 16 is in one sense quite clear; Jesus was certainly not ambiguous in his narrative. It just seems contrary to the character of Jesus to tell one like this. Praising what appeared to be unethical behavior or an unscrupulous person . . . the crowd didn't see *that* coming.

We have a hard time seeing it too. It just seems un-Christlike—or is it? Do we really understand the story? Do we really understand the Savior? The perceived lesson causes some distress; but then again, it's just like Jesus to surprise us. Here's how he told the story (Luke 16:1-7):

> There was a rich man whose manager was accused of wasting his possessions. So he called him in and asked him, "What is this I hear about you? Give an account of your management, because you cannot be manager any longer."
> The manager said to himself, "What shall I do now? My master is taking away my job. I'm not strong enough to dig, and I'm ashamed to beg—I know what I'll do so that, when I lose my job here, people will welcome me into their houses."
> So he called in each one of his master's debtors. He asked the first, "How much do you owe my master?"
> "Eight hundred gallons of olive oil," he replied.

The manager told him, "Take your bill, sit down quickly, and make it four hundred."

Then he asked the second, "And how much do you owe?"

"A thousand bushels of wheat," he replied.

He told him, "Take your bill and make it eight hundred."

What we know:

1. *A busy, wealthy man hired a manager to oversee his estate.* Probably not a slave, but someone skilled and trustworthy.

2. *According to custom, the manager's decisions were legally binding* (they would be regarded with the same weight as those of his master).[1]

3. *The manager, however, was accused of wasting his boss's money.* It was just an unsubstantiated allegation, but the employer heard about it, believed the report, and demanded an accounting of his manager's actions before his employment was terminated. Since the manager was likely the only person who knew the various accounts and financial obligations, he was given time to put the books in order and prepare his records.

With only a short time to prepare for a bleak future, the manager came up with a plan of action. In a moment of transparent self-examination, he concluded that he wasn't strong enough for manual labor, but he was too proud to beg. He summoned those who were indebted to the master and offered each the mother of all discounts.

Discount is a wonderful word, isn't it? Like me, you probably watch for sale flyers in the mail and discount coupons in the Sunday paper. Everyone loves a bargain. The steward knew his master's debtors would feel the same. Since the commodities in question were crops, it is likely these debtors were farming the master's land and owed him a portion of the profits.

These were not small debts. One man owed 800 gallons of olive oil (the yield of 150 olive trees, equal to three years' wages for an average day worker). So the manager offered him a clearance sale price of 50 percent off.

Another client owed 1,000 bushels of wheat (enough to feed 150 people for a year, equal to seven-and-a-half years' wages for an average day worker).[2] This debtor got the holiday sale price of 20 percent off.

Since the debtors accepted the discounts of 50 percent and 20 percent respectively, they became co-conspirators with the manager in his scheme. If needed, the manager had his blackmail backup plan. It is doubtful he would have stooped to such depths. In that day generosity carried with it the expectation that such deeds of kindness would be repaid.[3]

Lessons from an Unlikely Character

What came next in the parable is what muddies the water of understanding (Luke 16:8-12):

> The master commended the dishonest manager because he had acted shrewdly. For the people of this world are more shrewd in dealing with their own kind than are the people of the light. I tell you, use worldly wealth to gain friends for yourselves, so that when it is gone, you will be welcomed into eternal dwellings.
>
> Whoever can be trusted with very little can also be trusted with much, and whoever is dishonest with very little will also be dishonest with much. So if you have not been trustworthy in handling worldly wealth, who will trust you with true riches? And if you have not been trustworthy with someone else's property, who will give you property of your own?

Surprise! We shudder at the thought of Jesus using a shady character as a principle figure in his parable, and then *commending* him. But he obviously intended to teach us a valuable lesson, so let's be perceptive and see what we can glean from this topsy-turvy tale.

Hurry Up

Impetuous moves are frequently disastrous. There was nothing impulsive about this shrewd steward, however; his plan was calculated and timely. The steward had only a brief opportunity to prepare for the inevitable. Notice what he told the olive oil producer: "Take your bill, sit down quickly, and make it four hundred." Decisions were made swiftly, not carelessly. The steward perceptively considered his options, and then he acted decisively.

Too often we fail because we overanalyze a situation or get lost in the weeds of details. You will seldom have 100 percent of the information you need to make a perfect decision. Acting quickly and perceptively may make the difference between success and mediocrity. Dan Miller, in his book *48 Days to the Work You Love* references a Harvard Business School study on the top characteristics of high achievers: "Eighty percent of decisions should be made immediately."[4] The list included the obvious—intellect, education, attitude—but at the top of the list one characteristic stood out: speed of implementation. High achievers have the ability to act quickly.

> We shudder at the thought of Jesus using a shady character as a principle figure in his parable, and then *commending* him.

While not the key thought, the parable reminds us that there is a sense of urgency in our relationship with the Lord. Acknowledging Christ as Lord and Savior is a matter of utmost urgency. Sharing the gospel with those who haven't heard or who are spiritually negligent is an urgent need as well. We may lull ourselves into thinking we have all the time in the world to serve God, but we have no promise of more than this very moment. What can you do now that will make an eternal difference?

Wise Up

Perceptiveness can't be learned from a book; it's a type of wisdom one gains by surviving life. It's graduating from the school of hard knocks with a degree in common sense. Jesus made a startling judgment at the end of the parable—"For the people of this world are more shrewd in dealing with their own kind than are the people of the light" (v. 8). Sounds a bit insulting, doesn't it? What did Jesus mean by this comparison?

First, let's define the two groups. The "people of this world" are those whose focus in life does not include God. They live without the aid of his precepts or presence. The "people of the light" are those who follow Jesus, the Light of the world. They seek to reflect his light and imitate the character of Christ. The apostle Paul provided further insight in his letter to the church in Ephesus: "You were once darkness, but now you are light in the Lord. Live as children of light (for the fruit of the light consists in all goodness, righteousness and truth) and find out what pleases the Lord" (Ephesians 5:8-10).

The problem lies in the fact that sometimes God's people tend to be naïve. Jesus warned his followers against such naïveté: "Be as shrewd as snakes and as innocent as doves" (Matthew 10:16). It was a call to be perceptive—be street-smart but don't sin.

At some point in history the church abdicated its role as a leading cultural influence. I'm convinced the change was unintentional. It happened gradually, almost imperceptibly; but by the time it had become obvious, the "people of this world" had stepped in to fill the spiritual vacuum. Consequently, media outlets are in a better position to influence our current culture than the church is. Who has a better opportunity to shape the lives of our youth—the halls of academia or the church? In her efforts to imitate the gentleness of Christ, the church may have lost her sense of shrewd perception.

> Sometimes wisdom comes with age;
> sometimes age comes alone.

This parable issues a challenge to wise up. How do we become as perceptive as snakes and remain as gentle as doves? Consider these steps.

Pray for wisdom.
"If any of you lacks wisdom, he should ask God, who gives generously to all without finding fault, and it will be given to him. But when he asks, he must believe and not doubt, because he who doubts is like a wave of the

sea, blown and tossed by the wind" (James 1:5, 6). Prayer should be an obvious multilane highway to wisdom, but unfortunately, we often treat it like a forgotten back alley. Maybe that's why we children of the light aren't always as bright as we should be! James was also right when he wrote that we do not have because we do not ask (4:2). If you want to be wise in the eyes of God, start asking.

Work at wisdom.

I like the adage "Sometimes wisdom comes with age; sometimes age comes alone." The reason age sometimes comes alone is that we fail to work at being wiser. We just expect it to happen. Some morning you'll wake up and voilá—you're wise. It just doesn't work that way. Most skills are developed through disciplined practice, so work at being wise.

- Read the Bible and other challenging and informational books, periodicals, and articles.
- Analyze your mistakes so you won't repeat them.
- Visit with wise people; ask questions so you can learn from their experiences.
- Listen more than you talk.
- Don't assume you have all the answers.
- Explore both sides of any argument.
- Seek first to understand before you clamor to be understood.
- Be tenacious; wisdom is often gained through trial and error.

I like what American humorist Sam Levenson wrote: "It's so simple to be wise. Just think of something stupid to say and then don't say it."[5] I wish wisdom came so easily. Decide now to work at wisdom—don't let age come alone!

Grow in wisdom.

Be patient; occasionally the Lord grants wisdom—but mostly he teaches it. The teaching process takes longer but produces lasting results. When homeowners want quick shade for their yards, they often choose to plant silver maples. Unfortunately, the silver maple wood is soft, and within a few years the rapid growth gives way to broken limbs and split trunks in stormy weather. The wiser decision is to plant oak trees. The growth is much slower, but the stalwart oak will be around for generations to come. Be patient; let God grow his lasting wisdom in you.

Again, though this may not be the main thought, Jesus' words bring to mind a stinging realization: the people of this world give more thought to their physical well-being than the people of light do to their spiritual well-being. Ouch! If that is true—and I fear it may be for many of us—we really do need to wise up and change our focus. God wants us to be as perceptive about the spiritual as the world is preoccupied with the material.

Build Up

The perceptive manager took the occasion to build up relationships with those who could return the favor once he became jobless. Granted, he had an ulterior motive, but he was smart enough to know that he was going to need others if he intended to survive. Since most Christians are uncomfortable with the manager's behavior, alternative explanations have been offered to make the point a little more palatable. For instance:

- The steward didn't really cheat his master; he merely operated as the law specified. As the master's steward, his actions were regarded as legally binding, so if he wanted to discount the loans he could do so.
- The steward didn't really cheat his master; he only discounted his personal commission on the wheat and olive oil commodities.
- The steward didn't really cheat his master; he only eliminated interest on the loans to the wheat and olive farmers. And since interest was forbidden by the Mosaic law, he actually preserved his master's reputation and honored the law at the same time.

These are just rose-colored speculations. Nothing in the parable suggests that the master charged interest or that the steward was owed a commission. After all, Jesus did call the steward a "dirty, rotten, good-for-nothing scoundrel" (Ellsworth translation), so it is difficult to give him the benefit of the doubt.

Lloyd John Ogilvie said, "Our purpose is to use material resources as an expression of our friendship with God to make others His friends. That's the purpose of tithing and giving to Christian causes. Our money is used to support activities and programs that introduce people to the Saviour and care for their needs, in His name and for His glory."[6] I certainly have no issue with that description of a Christian's actions, but is that what Jesus was communicating? Read his application: "I tell you, use worldly wealth to gain friends for yourselves, so that when it is gone, you will be welcomed into eternal dwellings" (Luke 16:9).

> God wants us to be as perceptive about the spiritual as the world is preoccupied with the material.

Huh? Was Jesus really encouraging his followers to be deceptive or use ill-gotten money to buy friendship as a means to gain eternal favor? Are we to use money to buy friends in order to lead them to Heaven?

In discussing this difficult passage with my friend, Dr. John Ray, he offered another possibility. I'm intrigued by his insight from years of study and research. He concludes (as do other students of the Word) that Jesus used a somewhat ironic or cynical tone in verse nine that we miss in translation. Jesus certainly used irony at other times in his ministry, so it is conceivable that he was using it here. Rather than encouraging Christians to be as shrewd as the dishonest steward, he may have been using satire to make his point.

The thinking would go like this: Go ahead; follow the example of this ridiculous steward. Try to buy friendship using your ungodly riches. When the bottom falls out of your life, you can count on your purchased friends to provide you with an eternal home. Right? Oh, wait a minute . . . they have no eternal home to give you. . . .

Then again, it may just be that the interpretation is simpler than that. We tend to get sidetracked by comparing what a Christian ought to do with what this dishonest manager did. But Jesus never said we should imitate the *actions* of the guy. In the parable he is commended for being smart by the standards of his day. He used what resources had been entrusted to him to prepare for the future. His actions were, as Merriam-Webster defines it, "marked by clever discerning awareness" (*shrewd*).

The word *shrewd* makes us cringe. We often equate shrewd behavior with duplicitous behavior and therefore, dismiss it as a goal in Christian living. It may be helpful here to note that in ancient Mediterranean culture, shrewdness was an admirable quality—even if employed in ways that we might consider questionable. With this in mind, the master's commendation of his employee makes more sense. The employee was already known to be wasteful—that seems to be a given—but to demonstrate enough smarts to make the best of an awkward situation, this was a credit on his record.

So what about the message to the "people of the light"? We must not be guilty of the same actions, but we should be guided by a similar perceptive attitude. Are you shrewdly perceptive? Are your decisions about how you behave and what you do with the wealth you have been given "marked by clever discerning awareness"?

> Do what you say you will do; be who you claim to be.

True discernment will show us that one relationship matters more than all others—a relationship with the Lord. Invest your energies in building up *that* relationship. Only he can sustain you through the ups and downs of life. Only he can give you an eternal home in the kingdom of Heaven. But realize too that the way you behave toward others impacts the growth of that relationship with God, and vice versa. When we connect with the Lord first, then we are in a position to connect with others in a genuine way. True friendship can't be bought; it can only be built!

Show Up
Are you dependable? Do you have a reputation for being responsible? Can people trust you to show up when you have a job to do? Read again what Jesus said (vv. 10-12):

Whoever can be trusted with very little can also be trusted with much, and whoever is dishonest with very little will also be dishonest with much. So if you have not been trustworthy in handling worldly wealth, who will trust you with true riches? And if you have not been trustworthy with someone else's property, who will give you property of your own?

Understanding Jesus' point here doesn't require a degree in rocket science. If I ask you to help me with a project and you agree but fail to show (without explanation), I won't ask you again! Once a trust has been broken, it takes a lot of time and effort to reestablish it. Howard Hendricks gave his son some sage fatherly advice, "Be so dependable that if you say you will be somewhere and don't show up, they send flowers."[7] Dependability must have been on Jesus' mind when he said, "Simply let your 'Yes' be 'Yes' and your 'No,' 'No'" (Matthew 5:37). Do what you say you will do; be who you claim to be. God wants to use you in his kingdom, and he measures spiritual success not by the size of your role but by your reliability to carry out that role. Be trustworthy. When God calls, show up!

Stand Up

I grew up singing the old hymn "Stand Up, Stand Up for Jesus." It was one of those stir-your-passion kind of hymns, when the organist pulled out all the stops and the song leader always chided us, "You can't sing 'Stand Up for Jesus' while sittin' down!" So of course, we stood.

During my high school years, a cheer went up at every home basketball game: "Two bits, four bits, six bits, a dollar; all for our school stand up and holler." And we did.

When the U.S. national anthem, "The Star Spangled Banner," is sung or played, the country's citizens are asked to stand up as a demonstration of allegiance. And they do.

To *stand up* means you believe in and are dedicated to some person, purpose, or cause; it's your pledge to be faithfully committed. Jesus closed his remarks with these words: "No servant can serve two masters. Either he will hate the one and love the other, or he will be devoted to the one and despise the other. You cannot serve both God and Money" (v. 13).

A person cannot be committed to two opposing philosophies, ideals, or masters at the same time. That doesn't keep us from trying, but you can straddle the fence only so long before the barbed wire becomes a real pain. Occasionally, a story crops up in the news, exposing a man for being married to two wives at the same time, but separated by several states. Go figure! He's neither street-smart nor book-smart. James said, "He is a double-minded man, unstable in all he does" (1:8). The two-timer juggles the travel, support, and deceit as long as he can, but eventually truth wins out and he ends up a big loser.

As a culture, we struggle with commitment in multiple areas today.

- When you hear a couple exchange their vows with the words "so long as we both shall *love,*" it's appropriate to give a gift of disposable paper plates instead of heirloom china.
- Commitment between employers and employees used to be a cherished ideal, but today the average length of a job in America is only 3.2 years.[8]
- Elected officials change party allegiance if they believe such a move will be more advantageous in the next election.
- We sign multipage contracts full of legalese because a handshake and a promise don't mean much anymore.

It's no wonder so few people stand up for anything. In the kingdom of Heaven, however, commitment is everything. Jesus Christ willingly endured the rugged nails, thorny crown, rough-hewn wood, and the spiritual chasm created by sin, all because he was faithfully committed to our salvation. Yet we often compromise or even betray our commitment to him.

We are not so unlike the Pharisees, whom Jesus addressed at the end of his parable: "You are the ones who justify yourselves in the eyes of men, but God knows your hearts. What is highly valued among men is detestable in God's sight" (Luke 16:15).

I have the utmost respect for all branches of the military that truly understand what it means to be committed to a cause. Of all their mottoes, the Marines' *Semper Fidelis* resonates best with the follower of Christ— "Always Faithful." That may well be the best definition of *commitment*.

> A person cannot be committed to two opposing philosophies, ideals, or masters at the same time.

Of all the monuments in and around our nation's capital, the Marine Corps War Memorial holds the distinction of being one of the largest bronze statutes ever cast. Modeled after the famous photo snapped by war correspondent Joe Rosenthal, it depicts the soldiers who raised the American flag atop Mt. Suribachi on the island of Iwo Jima. To see the statue lit at night is breathtaking.

Several years ago while our family was in Washington, D.C., I stopped to browse at a sidewalk souvenir stand. On the table was a small brass replica of the Marine Corps War Memorial. I picked it up, and the man behind the counter must have sensed an impending sale. "Cheap," he said, "it's only $10." I held the miniature sculpture and thought, *Cheap! There was nothing cheap about this moment in history—just ask the marines who landed there in February of 1945 and witnessed one of the costliest battles of World War II.* Thirty-five days later, 6,821 U.S. military personnel had given their lives for this tiny piece of real estate, and more than 20,000 had been wounded.[9] These courageous men were willing to stand up and be counted for our country. That's commitment; always faithful!

Can Jesus, who gave all for us, depend on us to stand up and be faithful for him?

1. Take an honest look at yourself—what percentage of your thinking comes from book smarts as compared to street smarts? Which knowledge has been more valuable? more practical? Why?

2. "We may lull ourselves into thinking we have all the time in the world to serve God, but we have no promise of more than this very moment." Make a list of the urgent matters of the kingdom of God. On a scale of one to ten, with one being low, how would you rate your sense of urgency for spiritual matters? From your perspective, what should be the most urgent priority of the church? Why?

3. "Perceptiveness can't be learned from a book; it's a type of wisdom one gains by surviving life. It's graduating from the school of hard knocks with a degree in common sense." What practical things can you do to enhance wisdom in your life? How do you pray for wisdom?

Didn't See That Coming
For individual or group study

4. "True discernment will show us that one relationship matters more than all others—a relationship with the Lord." In what specific ways do you work on your relationship with the Lord? What have you found to be the most successful tools as you grow in the Lord?

5. "Whoever can be trusted with very little can also be trusted with much, and whoever is dishonest with very little will also be dishonest with much." How do you know if people consider you dependable? Can people trust you to show up when you have a job to do? Why or why not?

6. "A person cannot be committed to two opposing philosophies, ideals, or masters at the same time." What are some examples in which people try to be committed to opposite ideas at the same time? Have you ever tried to straddle the proverbial fence, and if so, what was the result? How can you best stand up for Jesus where you live and work?

Love, though said to be afflicted with blindness,
is a vigilant watchman.
—Charles Dickens, *Our Mutual Friend*

At the Tomb of the Unknown Soldier in Arlington Cemetery, posted signs urge visitors to remain silent. Those signs seem unnecessary; who could talk in the presence of such vigilant reverence? Carved on the white marble sarcophagus are these words: "Here rests in honored glory an American soldier known but to God."

Unidentified remains of soldiers from WWI, WWII, and the Korean War lie in their crypts while an elite honor guard keeps vigil around the clock.[1] Words fail to capture the inspirational image of those who guard the tomb. It is considered a sacred honor to serve as one of the tomb's sentinels. To hear taps played or to witness the changing of the guard is both moving and thrilling at the same time. Each sentinel stands in four positions during his walk. He begins at the end of the black walking mat by facing the tomb for twenty-one seconds. He then turns toward the opposite end, clicks his heels, changes the rifle to his shoulder farthest from the tomb (signifying

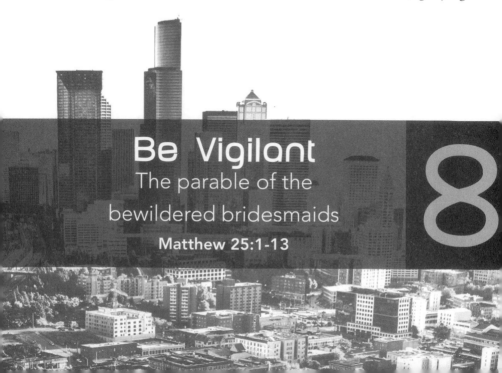

Be Vigilant
The parable of the bewildered bridesmaids
Matthew 25:1-13

8

his duty to guard it), stands again for twenty-one seconds, and then takes exactly twenty-one steps to the end, where the whole ritual is repeated. Each segment of twenty-one represents a twenty-one gun salute.

> The happy occasion is a wedding;
> the tragic conclusion is a warning.

The Tomb of the Unknown Soldier has been guarded continuously, twenty-four hours a day, seven days a week, since July 2, 1937. While provision is made for the sentinel's protection in inclement weather, nothing has ever deterred the honor guard from its sacred duty. I love the motto shared by those who have guarded this tomb: "Soldiers never die until they are forgotten."

Tomb guards never forget.

I know of no better definition or demonstration of vigilance.

A Wedding Story

Matthew recorded a surprising parable that Jesus, in the closing days of his earthly ministry, told to challenge his followers to be vigilant. The happy occasion is a wedding; the tragic conclusion is a warning (Matthew 25:1-13):

> At that time the kingdom of heaven will be like ten virgins who took their lamps and went out to meet the bridegroom. Five of them were foolish and five were wise. The foolish ones took their lamps but did not take any oil with them. The wise, however, took oil in jars along with their lamps. The bridegroom was a long time in coming, and they all became drowsy and fell asleep.
>
> At midnight the cry rang out: "Here's the bridegroom! Come out to meet him!"
>
> Then all the virgins woke up and trimmed their lamps. The foolish ones said to the wise, "Give us some of your oil; our lamps are going out."

"No," they replied, "there may not be enough for both us and you. Instead, go to those who sell oil and buy some for yourselves."

But while they were on their way to buy the oil, the bridegroom arrived. The virgins who were ready went in with him to the wedding banquet. And the door was shut.

Later the others also came. "Sir! Sir!" they said. "Open the door for us!"

But he replied, "I tell you the truth, I don't know you."

Therefore keep watch, because you do not know the day or the hour.

Planning the Perfect Wedding

The customs of first-century weddings were very different from today's practices. To fully appreciate this powerful message about vigilance, we need to view the parable through the lens of a first-century Jewish marriage. So forget everything you know about a traditional American wedding: aisle runners, flower girls, and unity candles.

Today brides and their families may spend a few months preparing for the big day, but in first-century Jewish culture, the planning began *years* before. Though there were exceptions, most marriages were arranged by the parents. Part of that arrangement involved the *mohar*—the price paid by the groom's family to the bride's father for the loss of his daughter (a custom I regret is no longer in practice!). A coin or something of value was given to the bride at the time of the contract if she indeed agreed to the upcoming marriage. This was hers to keep; a token or seal of the commitment—much like an engagement ring.[2]

A first-century marriage went through two stages: betrothal and the actual marriage ceremony. The betrothal period was a legally binding promise of marriage. During this first stage, which could last up to a year, a betrothed man was exempt from military service. A betrothed woman was regarded as if already married; any man who violated her during her betrothal was stoned as an adulterer. And as you might expect, the beginning of this engagement period was marked with feasts and celebrations.

The actual marriage ceremony was called the huppah, or canopy. The entire community celebrated this weeklong festival with the bride and groom. The groom made the first move. In his own time and accompanied by his friends, he made his way to the bride's house, where the ceremony began. Nighttime was often preferred; it heightened the element of surprise. It was considered a crass insult to decline a wedding invitation, so an evening wedding made it much easier for guests to attend after finishing their labors of the day.[3]

Since no one in the bride's household knew exactly what time the bridegroom and his entourage might arrive, the bridal party was compelled to be ready. At any moment they might hear the best man announce his approach with a shout. The groom would then take his veiled bride and, together with her friends and family, journey to his house where the festivities began.

Obviously, street lamps were nonexistent, so the bridesmaids (customarily ten in number) would light the way. Some suggest that the bridesmaids in the parable were carrying small clay lamps that held only a small amount of oil, but these lamps produced such little light that they could hardly have guided the wedding party to its destination. It is more likely that these bridesmaids carried oil-soaked rag torches that had to be refreshed with olive oil every few minutes. The torches, however, would have lit the path more clearly, ensuring the safe arrival of the bride and groom.[4]

> No one knew exactly what time the bridegroom might arrive; the bridal party was compelled to be ready.

As they proceeded through the streets, love songs accompanied their walk, poetry was recited, and speeches were given in honor of the special couple. People looked down from the flat-roofed houses and shouted their joyful encouragement as the wedding party made its way through the night.

For seven days the bride and groom did no work, wore their festal clothing, and were considered king and queen of the festivities. For the most part, the couple did not participate in the games of celebration, but were mere observers as others celebrated in their honor. Considered the social events of the year, wedding celebrations were cherished by the whole community.[5]

They Failed to Plan

I have many fun memories from weddings I've performed through the years of my ministry. I've witnessed a couple leave in a hot-air balloon from the front lawn of the church; a ring bearer who collapsed, toppling the flower stands like dominoes; a groom or two who needed a chair to make it through the ceremony; and a Labrador retriever that served as best man. The solid black Lab sported a white bow tie and was the best-behaved best man I've ever worked with.

At the end of one wedding rehearsal, a somewhat bewildered bride-to-be said to me, "You left out the part where you put us under." She could see the puzzled look in my eye and went on, "You know . . . when we kiss . . . you're supposed to put us under." Then it dawned on me; she was talking about the traditional charge given to the wedded couple: "What God has joined together, let no man *put asunder*." I worried a lot about that marriage!

But in all the weddings I've performed, I've never witnessed anything as disastrous as what happened in Jesus' parable. These young women made a serious error in judgment—such a flippant attitude and lack of protocol was inexcusable. They failed the bride and the groom; they failed to be vigilant. The crowd would have been shocked. They didn't see *that* one coming.

What does Jesus intend for us to learn from this wedding story? Vigilance, as spelled out in this parable, is comprised of three concepts: preparation, watchfulness, and devotion.

Preparation

As is true of weddings today, it was a great honor to be chosen by the bride to serve as one of her attendants. Today it is more honorary than necessary; in that day the young ladies had the responsibility of providing light from the bride's house to the couple's new home. It certainly required preparation—a working torch or lamp, a means to light the torch, and plenty of oil to keep the torch burning, since no one could be certain when the groom would arrive. Historians estimate that rag torches would have burned about fifteen minutes before they needed replenishing.[6] If the bridesmaids waited a few hours for the groom to arrive and kept their torches burning during that time, extra oil would have been required. To show up with only the oil in their torch rags would have been foolish at best, if not insulting to the bride and groom.

In the parable a tardy groom—maybe extra nervous or mischievous—delayed his coming for so long that five of the bridesmaids ran out of oil. They begged for some oil from the well-prepared other five, but they refused to share. Some who read this parable are indignant at such selfish behavior. But had they shared, none would have had enough oil, the torches would have become nothing but smoldering rags, and the bridal party would have been left in the dark.

Consequently, the foolish ones hurried off in search of a merchant to buy more oil. There was no such thing as a twenty-four-hour Walmart in those days. Finding a merchant in the community who had not been invited to the wedding would have been difficult; and if they did find one, persuading him to get out of bed at midnight and open his shop would have been even harder. By the time the ill-equipped bridesmaids showed up at the groom's house, the wedding was in full swing, the door was bolted, and they were turned away.

How foolish not to prepare for the inevitable!

Preparation in most areas of life is vital. I remember well my first flight lesson, June 12, 1973. I was really pumped. I couldn't wait to get into the air. As my instructor and I reached the plane, I started for the Piper Cherokee's single door, but he stopped me. "We have to do a preflight," he barked. *A what?* If this is some kind of pep talk, I don't need it. I'm already so excited my goose bumps are hugging each other. He went on to explain the instructional checklist that a pilot must follow before he even settles into the cockpit. We checked for condensation in the fuel tanks; the proper level of oil in the engine crankcase; freedom of movement in the ailerons, rudder, and elevator; damage to the brake lines; properly inflated tires; evidence of a bird nesting in the cowling—and on the list went. He spent forty-five minutes teaching me how to prepare the airplane for flight before we climbed aboard. I learned a valuable lesson that day on the importance of preparation. When it comes to flying, cross every *t* and dot every *i* while the plane is still on the ground. It's a little difficult to check for fuel tank condensation or low oil once in the air.

> The most important area of preparation in life often goes overlooked: spiritual preparation.

We understand the importance of preparation in many areas.

- We prepare for a career through education or apprenticeships.
- We prepare for surgery through various tests and procedures designed to isolate the problem.
- We prepare for the birth of a child through doctor visits, a healthy lifestyle, and securing the necessary items for a new family member: cradle, bottles, blankets, diapers, clothes, baby lotions, etc.
- We prepare to buy a house through hours of looking, title searches, loan applications, negotiating closing costs, collecting boxes, moving vans, and gathering good friends to help with the process.

No one would argue with any of these areas, but the most important area of preparation in life often goes overlooked: spiritual preparation. I know sincere nonbelievers who are convinced that God's goodness will compel him to overlook their faults. After all, they reason, they are just as good as many Christians they know—if not better. But it's never about our goodness or God overlooking our faults; it's about trusting Jesus who paid the sacrificial price to rid us of our sins. These same folks wouldn't think of buying a house without a deed, having surgery without a sterile operating room, or flying across the country without a licensed pilot. Yet they nonchalantly face eternity without a Savior.

This parable was part of Jesus' answer to questions about the end of time. The parable began with the words "At *that* time." *That* references a time yet to come. Perhaps Paul was thinking of this parable when he wrote to the Thessalonian Christians about the Lord's return in 1 Thessalonians 4:13–5:11. The parallels are striking. As with the bridesmaids and the approaching groom, you won't know the exact time Jesus is coming. So be prepared! Don't get left out of the celebration.

Watchfulness

Showing up later than sooner was not all that uncommon. Grooms took great pleasure in the element of surprise or in finding the bridal party sleeping. In this parable the element of delay is significant—it reminds us what can happen when one fails to watch. Being watchful carries with it a twofold challenge: to stay alert and to keep your guard up.

Alertness maintains focus. Have you ever started daydreaming in the middle of a conversation when suddenly you hear the other person call your name and repeat a question? It jars you back to reality, but you have no idea how to answer the question because you checked out on the conversation long ago. You lost focus—you weren't alert or watchful. Now you feel embarrassed and the other person is slightly insulted.

> Being watchful carries with it a twofold challenge:
> to stay alert and to keep your guard up.

There is a big push in society to stem the tide of drivers who e-mail or text while behind the wheel. Why? Because you aren't as alert—you lose focus when you're looking at your phone instead of the road. It's dangerous for both you and others on the road. This message appeared recently on a church marquee: "Honk if you love Jesus; text while driving if you want to meet him."

It's easy to lose focus on Jesus' promise to return. When you are distracted by the temporal instead of the eternal, it's easy to take your eyes off the road home. After all, life feels routine. Every morning the sun comes up as usual. We head to work, break for lunch, work some more, return home in the evening, go to bed, and repeat the whole thing the next day. We rationalize: *I've got time; he hasn't come for 2,000 years. I'm healthy. Death is a long way off. . .* We doze spiritually. And while we are slumbering our way through life, we let down our guard. And that's when our enemy takes advantage. "Be sober, be vigilant; because your adversary the devil walks about like a roaring lion, seeking whom he may devour" (1 Peter 5:8, *NKJV*).

In April 2009, the findings of a new investigative study into the Great Wall of China revealed that, at its longest, the wall stretched 5,500 miles. The entire wall no longer remains today, but at its height of usefulness, the wall supported 723 beacon towers; 7,062 lookout towers; 3,357 wall platforms; and 1,026 other ruins.[7] Millions of laborers died during the centuries it took to complete it. In 1644, however, the Manchurian army finally breached the Great Wall, not by scaling it or breaking through, but by bribing an important general, Wu Sangui, who for a price opened the gates of Shanhai Pass and allowed the Manchurians into China.[8]

I don't care how strong your resolve may be; when you let down your guard, it's like opening the gates to let the enemy into your life. A little compromise here, a little yielding there, and suddenly the walls of your resolve are breached.

In the context of this parable Jesus reminded his disciples—and us too—that his coming would not necessarily be immediate. Since a day is like a thousand years with the Lord, his return could seem delayed by our standards, all the while being very much on target according to God's plan. Stay alert. Keep your guard up. Be focused. I like the expression Shooter used in the classic basketball movie *Hoosiers*, when he called the picket fence play at the end of the game: "Now boys, don't get caught watching the paint dry."

The Gospel of Mark records another parable with the same intent:

No one knows about that day or hour, not even the angels in heaven, nor the Son, but only the Father. Be on guard! Be alert!

You do not know when that time will come. It's like a man going away: He leaves his house and puts his servants in charge, each with his assigned task, and tells the one at the door to keep watch.

Therefore keep watch because you do not know when the owner of the house will come back—whether in the evening, or at midnight, or when the rooster crows, or at dawn. If he comes suddenly, do not let him find you sleeping. What I say to you, I say to everyone: "Watch!" (Mark 13:32-37)

Devotion

Reality television shows have become a popular part of our viewing options, and many of the shows revolve around marriage: *A Wedding Story, For Better or For Worse, Whose Wedding Is It Anyway?* and more. I find it sadly interesting that in the fourteen seasons of *The Bachelor*, not one bachelor is still married to or even dating the young lady to whom he proposed on the show's climactic episode.[9] Few such productions are built around the one element that is vital to marital success—lasting devotion to one another. This parable gives us one more incredible insight into the Savior's heart: his loving devotion to his bride the church. He will come for her, and that's a promise.

In a day when so many are dismissively critical of the church, I want us to remember that for all her human warts and blemishes, she is still the bride of Christ and he loves her dearly. Is it even possible to love the Savior without loving his bride? The end of the parable would suggest not. "Later the others also came. 'Sir! Sir!' they said. 'Open the door for us!' But he replied, 'I tell you the truth, I don't know you'" (vv. 11, 12). Of this I am sure: the Lord will know you if you are in love with his bride.

The bride

She stepped out of the bridal room into the back hallway behind the worship center. It was my first glimpse of her dressed for her wedding day. I think she heard me catch my breath.

"Dad, are you all right?"

"Sure," I lied, but the tears betrayed my deceit. What a glorious sight! How could I even think of giving someone so beautiful . . . so special . . . so precious . . . away to another man?

There is something uniquely special about the bride.

I've heard that in the split second before a life-threatening accident, time stands still and the scenes from one's entire life parade before the eyes. There was no impending accident in that back hallway, but for a moment time stood still. It wasn't my life, but hers that flashed past my teary eyes. I saw the doctor placing her into my trembling arms in those first breathless moments of life (I was breathless, she wasn't). The next images came at me furiously—tumbling one after the other to the forefront of my mind, not giving me nearly enough time to savor each memory before it was replaced with another just as treasured:

- The Christmas morning she awoke with chicken pox.
- Her big-wheel tricycle that she rode *everywhere.*
- The morning she didn't let me walk her to the door of her kindergarten classroom because I was wearing work overalls on my day off.
- The trips we shared to revivals and how she'd sit on the front pew coloring a picture—patiently waiting for me to conclude my sermon.
- The evening she wore a wedding dress as Tevye's daughter Tzeitel in her high school's production of *Fiddler on the Roof.*
- The whoops of joy when she mastered a manual transmission.
- The moment she fell into my arms sobbing after she lost her state tennis match.

"Dad," she probed, "how do I look?" The question jolted me back from my sentimental journey.

"Absolutely beautiful!"

Words can be so inadequate at times. How can a father express the inexpressible? Everyone around her faded from view, and I saw this indescribable vision of the woman who had only moments before been my little girl. Her radiant image is permanently glued in my mind's scrapbook of all-time favorite memories.

There is something uniquely special about the bride. Like honeybees crowded around the hive, her attendants helped her with the finishing touches. I smiled as they giggled together, and I thought, *What is it that makes a wedding so special?* I have been privileged to perform dozens of ceremonies for wonderful couples through my years in ministry, and each is memorable. Some, however, don't start out that way.

I'll admit that weddings occasionally become more of a job than a joy. As some well-intentioned, second-rate musician plunks her way through "Canon in D"—causing Pachelbel to spin in his grave—I view my role as simply another ministerial duty. I realize that may sound harsh, but for a moment just stop and consider the average wedding ceremony from my perspective. The order of service varies little:

- Parents
- Parson
- Processional
- Prayers
- Promises
- Performer
- Pronouncement
- Postlude

See what I mean? After a while the music sounds the same, the rings sparkle the same, the flowers smell the same, and the candles are still hard to light. And let's be honest; there is nothing really special about those of us who have been grooms. If you've seen one glassy-eyed groom in an overpriced tux, you've seen them all.

If you could stand where I stand, you might understand why I'm sometimes joy-challenged. Taking my place at the front, I look out over the assembled guests. I notice that most of the women seem a bit tearful, while most of the men just seem bored to tears. The bridal entourage parades down the aisle, and if the crowd is lucky, the ring bearer will do something totally unpredictable, much to the chagrin of his mother in the third row. It's all so predictable up to this point.

Then everything changes. Music swells and anticipation rushes into the room. The bride's mother stands and turns to face the back of the room. The doors swing open. What just a moment ago seemed so ordinary is suddenly transformed into something extraordinary. The crowd rises to its feet, I stand a little taller, and the groom loses that deer-in-the-headlights expression as he falls in love with her all over again. You see, the bride makes all the difference. And by the time she and her father have reached the end of the aisle, I have once again lost myself in the wonder of it all.

> What just a moment ago seemed so ordinary is suddenly transformed into something extraordinary.

The Bride

Of all the terms Jesus used to describe his church, *bride* is my favorite. Surprisingly, it is John the Baptist who introduces us to the concept. When Jesus' ministry began to overshadow John's, his disciples became a bit indignant. John set them straight: "You yourselves can testify that I said, 'I am not the Christ but am sent ahead of him.' The bride belongs to the bridegroom. The friend who attends the bridegroom waits and listens for him, and is full of joy when he hears the bridegroom's voice. That joy is mine, and it is now complete. He must become greater; I must become less" (John 3:28-30).

Throughout his entire ministry John had played the role of a groomsman—the Best Man. He had been preparing the way for the coming of the divine Groom.

Jesus used a similar analogy throughout his life and teaching. His first miracle—initiating his earthly ministry—didn't occur at the temple or by the seashore, but at a wedding banquet. Evidently someone in the groom's family miscalculated the amount of wine needed, and the wine ran out while the celebration was in full swing. Sparing the groom and bride any embarrassment, Jesus took ordinary water, turned it into exquisite wine, and saved the day. The guests could not have known the significance of that moment, but Jesus knew. In a mere three years his blood, like that exquisite wine, would be poured out to save forever his bride, the church.

> As a bride is loved and adored, so should we love and cherish the church with all our hearts.

The Parable of the Ten Bridesmaids isn't the only wedding-themed parable that Jesus told. Earlier in his ministry he told a captivating story of a grand wedding banquet where the bridal party was assembled, but none of the invited guests had shown up. The father of the groom quickly sent his servants to every nook and cranny in the community to invite anyone and everyone to the feast. Shortly, the hall filled to capacity. People from all walks of life and all levels of society joined together to celebrate the grand wedding that so many rudely dismissed as inconsequential. What an insult!

You too have been invited by the heavenly Father to share in the wedding celebration of his Son. Miss whatever you must, but don't miss this grand wedding of eternity.

The analogy doesn't end there. We are reminded of Jesus' incredible love for his bride as the apostle Paul wrote to the Ephesian Christians. In his letter he challenged the men to love their brides "just as Christ loved the church and gave himself up for her" (Ephesians 5:25). If every married man could incorporate that one single example into his role as husband, it would transform marriage today.

If John the Baptist, the apostle Paul, and especially the Lord Jesus all viewed the church as the bride, then what does that convey to us about the priceless nature of the kingdom?

- As a bride appears in her finest on her wedding day, so should we do our best to make the church always look beautiful through our actions and words.
- As a bride is loved and adored, so should we love and cherish the church with all our hearts.
- As a bride leaves her home to join her groom and make a new life with him, so should we leave behind the world and all that is in it to make a new life with Christ.
- As a bride forsakes all others, so must we be faithful and devoted only to Jesus.

To receive an invitation to a wedding is indeed an honor. Some invitations are rather simple; others are extravagant. All should be viewed as a privilege. And so it is when we come to the last chapter of John's Revelation. We are presented with the most glorious wedding invitation ever: "The Spirit and the bride say, 'Come!'" (22:17). Will you RSVP to that invitation? Are you making plans to be there? Are you devoted to the Groom with all your heart, soul, mind, and strength?

Even now, preparations are being made. All of Heaven is looking forward to that day. You have a place at the table if you want it. Get dressed—this is one glorious occasion for which you'll want to look your finest. When that day arrives the trumpet music will swell, the doors of Heaven will swing open, and the Bride will be carried over the threshold of eternity. While you wait for that day and the first glimpse of his appearing, the Groom desperately wants you to fall in love with his Bride, the church!

"Dad, are you ready?" she whispered. The day had passed so quickly, but there we were, the last two standing at the back of the worship center. Everyone was in place. She squeezed my arm and grinned. I melted. The music swelled, the doors swung open, and I saw *my* bride stand and turn to watch our daughter enter. As we stepped through the open doors and into her grand moment, I glanced once more at my daughter and thought, *Oh, how I love the bride!*

1. How would you describe what *vigilance* means? From your experience is it a practiced virtue of the Christian life? Why or why not? Why is it important?

2. "I know sincere nonbelievers who are convinced that God's goodness will compel him to overlook their faults. After all, they reason, they are just as good as many Christians they know—if not better." How do you think our society compares to that of Jesus' day in the area of spiritual preparedness? Where do you think the idea developed that "being good" is the same as being prepared? How can we help others change their understanding of being prepared for eternity?

3. "Being watchful carries with it a twofold challenge: to stay alert and to keep your guard up." What do you do to stay spiritually alert? List some ways you can guard against the enemy's attack. What are some of the distractions in life that cause us to lose spiritual focus?

Didn't See That Coming
For individual or group study

4. "In a day when so many are dismissively critical of the church, I want us to remember that for all her human warts and blemishes, she is still the bride of Christ and he loves her dearly." Is it even possible to love the Savior without loving his bride? Why are so many (including Christians) critical of the church today? What part of the criticism has merit? What part doesn't? Explain your answer.

5. What practical things can you do to demonstrate your devotion to the Lord's bride, the church?

Introduction

1. Klyne R. Snodgrass, *Stories with Intent* (Grand Rapids: William B. Eerdmans Publishing Co., 2008), 7.

2. Simon J. Kistemaker, *The Parables* (Grand Rapids: Baker Books, 1980), 9–10.

3. Herbert Lockyer, *All the Parables of the Bible* (Grand Rapids: Zondervan Publishing House, 1963), 144.

4. Lloyd John Ogilvie, *Autobiography of God* (Ventura: Regal Books, 1979), 7.

Chapter 1

Epigraph: Deborah DeFord, ed., *Quotable Quotes* (Pleasantville, NY: The Reader's Digest Association, Inc., 1997), 81.

1. "Denarius," http://en.wikipedia.org/wiki/Denarius (accessed 6/28/2010).

2. Brent Kessel, "How Much Money Is Enough?" http://articles.moneycentral.msn.com/Investing/StockInvestingTrading/HowMuchMoneyIsEnough.aspx (accessed 4/19/2010).

3. Leo Tolstoy, "How Much Land Does a Man Need?" http://www.katinkahesselink.net/other/tolstoy.html (accessed 4/14/2010).

4. DeFord, 42.

Notes

Chapter 2

Epigraph: Frederick Buechner, "Wishful Thinking" (New York: Harper and Row Publishers, 1973).

1. Ikimulisa Livingston, John Doyle, and Dan Mangan, "Stabbed Hero Dies as More Than 20 People Stroll Past Him," http://www.nypost.com/p/news/local/queens/passers_by_let_good_sam_die_5SGkf5XDP5ooudVuEd8fbI (accessed 5/10/2010).

2. Mark Moore, *The Chronological Life of Christ,* Vol. 1 (Joplin: College Press Publishing Company, 1996), 411.

3. "Two Great Saves," *People Magazine*, February 20, 2006, Vol. 65, No. 7, http://www.people.com/people/archive/article/0,,20156851,00.html (accessed 5/11/2010).

4. http://www.sermoncentral.com/Illustrations/SearchResults.asp?Category=&Page=2&Sort=rank&keyword=compassion&AdvancedSearch=1&ExactPhrase=&OrKeyword1=&OrKeyword2=&OrKeyword3=&WordsToExclude=&ScriptureBookA2=&ScriptureVerse=&TopicID=0&since2=0&Submitted2=1.

Chapter 3

Epigraph: Stormie Omartian, *Seven Prayers That Will Change Your Life Forever* (Nashville: Thomas Nelson, 2006), 47.

1. Craig S. Keener, *IVP Bible Background Commentary: New Testament* (Downers Grove: InterVarsity Press, 1993), 235.

2. Morris Womack, *Learning to Live from the Parables* (Joplin: College Press Publishing Company, 1995), 191.

3. Moore, Vol. 1, 361–362.

4. William Barclay, *New Testament Words* (Louisville, KY: Westminster John Knox Press, 1974).

5. Robert C. Shannon, *1000 Windows* (Cincinnati: Standard Publishing, 1997), 89.

6. H. C. Leupold, *Exposition of Genesis,* Vol. 1 (Grand Rapids: Baker Book House, 1942), 222–224.

7. John Ortberg, *Everybody's Normal Till You Get to Know Them* (Grand Rapids: Zondervan, 2003), 158–159.

Chapter 4

Epigraph: from Edward K. Rowell, editor, *Quotes and Idea Starters for Preaching and Teaching* (Grand Rapids: Baker Books, 1996), 73.

1. Mark E. Moore, *The Chronological Life of Christ,* Vol. 2 (Joplin: College Press Publishing Company, 1997), 51.

2. Merrill C. Tenney, ed., "Decapolis," *The Zondervan Pictorial Encyclopedia of the Bible,* Vol. 2 (Grand Rapids: Zondervan Publishing House, 1978), 81–84.

3. The Life of Jesus in the History of LEGIO X FRETENSIS, http://www.home.surewest.net/fifi/index22.htm (accessed 4/20/2010). And see *The Journal of Greco-Roman Christianity and Judaism*, Vol. 1, 2000 (Sheffield, UK: Sheffield Phoenix Press, 2004), 208.

4. "Robbers Call Bank for Money to Go," http://www.huffingtonpost.com/2010/03/24/robbers-call-bank-formon_n_511303.html (accessed 3/10/2010).

5. To read more about Dr. Cottrell's thoughts on grace, see his book *What the Bible Says About Grace: Set Free!* (Joplin: College Press, 2009).

6. Quoted in Moore, Vol. 2, 68.

7. Ibid., 69.

Chapter 5

Epigraph: *Webster's Book of Quotations* (New York: PMC Publishing Company, 1994), 99.

1. Merrill C. Tenney, ed., *The Zondervan Pictorial Encyclopedia of the Bible*, Vol. 3 (Grand Rapids: Zondervan Publishing House, 1976), 138–140.

2. Craig S. Keener, *IVP Bible Background Commentary: New Testament* (Downers Grove: InterVarsity Press, 1993), 242.

3. Ibid.

4. Alexis Kashar, "Have We Lulled Ourselves into Complacency?" http://www
.nad.org/blogs/alexiskashar/have-we-lulled-ourselves-complacency (accessed
5/24/2010).

Chapter 6
Epigraph: DeFord, 97.

1. D. A. Hagner, "Pharisee," *The Zondervan Pictorial Encyclopedia of the Bible*,
Vol. 4, Merrill C. Tenney, ed. (Grand Rapids: Zondervan Publishing House,
1976), 745–752.

2. http://www.getamused.com/jokes/irsjokes.html (accessed 6/19/2010).

3. "Historic Jesus: Tax Collector," http://www.historicjesus.com/character/tax
collectors.html.

4. Charles R. Swindoll, *The Tale of the Tardy Oxcart* (Nashville: Word Publishing, 1998), 278.

5. John Wooden, *Wooden* (Lincolnwood: Contemporary Books, 1997), 198.

6. Moore, Vol. 2, 103.

7. Ibid., 103.

Chapter 7
Epigraph: *The Free Dictionary*, http://www.thefreedictionary.com/street%20
smart (accessed 4/22/2010).

1. Snodgrass, 406.

2. Ibid.

3. Ibid.

4. Dan Miller, *48 Days to the Work You Love* (Nashville: Broadman & Holman
Publishers, 2005), 55.

5. *Reader's Digest*, September 2004, 111.

6. Lloyd John Ogilvie, *Autobiography of God* (Ventura: Regal Books, 1979),
205.

7. Raymond McHenry, *The Best of In Other Words* (Houston: Raymond McHenry Publisher, 1996), 69.

8. Miller, 20.

9. "Marines Land on Iwo Jima," http://www.marines.mil/unit/mcbbutler/Pages/2006/MWHS-1%20Marines%20land%20on%20Iwo%20Jima.aspx (accessed 6/27/2010).

Chapter 8

Epigraph: Charles Dickens, *Our Mutual Friend* (Philadelphia: T. B. Peterson & Brothers, 1865), 154.

1. "Tomb Guard," http://tombguard.org/site.html.

2. Merrill C. Tenney, "Marriage" *The Zondervan Pictorial Encyclopedia of the Bible*, Vol. 4 (Grand Rapids: Zondervan Publishing House, 1976). 96.

3. Ibid., 96–97.

4. Kistemaker, 114.

5. Tenney, "Marriage," 97.

6. Kistemaker, 114–115.

7. Great Wall of China, http://www.travelchinaguide.com/china_great_wall/facts/how-long.htm (accessed 6/26/2010).

8. "Great Wall Breached," http://www.kinabaloo.com/great_wall.html (accessed 6/26/2010).

9. "The Bachelor," http://en.wikipedia.org/wiki/The_Bachelor_(TV_series) (accessed 6/24/2010).

Tom Ellsworth has served as the preaching minister at Sherwood Oaks Christian Church in Bloomington, Indiana, since 1981. In his free time, he enjoys aviation history and tinkering with his 1948 Chrysler. Mostly he loves spending time with his wife, Elsie, and their two grown daughters, together with their families. Tom is also the author of the Standard Publishing resources *It's Your Move—On Board, It's Your Move—Out Loud,* and *Beyond Your Backyard* (with *Beyond Your Backyard Group Member Discussion Guide*), and co-authored *Preaching James* (Chalice Press).

Tom loves to hear from readers! To contact him, or for more information about his writing ministry, visit: www.tdellsworth.com.

About the Author

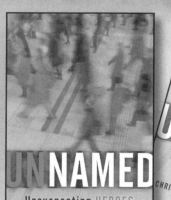